Networking
with
Microcomputers

Colin Pye

PUBLISHED BY NCC PUBLICATIONS

British Library Cataloguing in Publication Data

Pye, C.
    Networking with microcomputers.
    1. Computer networks.   2. Microcomputers
    I. Title   II. National Computing Centre
    001.64'404   TK5105.5

    ISBN 0-85012-468-9

To my wife, Margaret, and our parents

First published in 1985 by:

NCC Publications, The National Computing Centre Limited, Oxford Road, Manchester, M1 7ED, England.

Typeset in 11pt Times Roman by UPS Blackburn Limited, 76-80 Northgate, Blackburn, Lancashire; and printed by Hobbs the Printers of Southampton.

ISBN 0-85012-468-9

Acknowledgements

The author wishes to thank the following organisations for their literature and help in the preparation of this book:

Acorn Computers Limited
ACT (UK) Limited
Autodata
British Paper & Board Federation
Data Exchange
Digital Microsystems
Digitus
Fisons
Future Computers
Inland Revenue
International Business Machines
International Computers Limited
Manchester University
Metal Box Company Limited
Quorum Computers Limited
Racal-Milgo Limited
Semiconductor Specialists (UK) Limited
Sterling Computer Services
Torch Computers

The author would also like to thank NCC colleagues for their advice and comments on the text:

K. C. E. Gee
E. V. Bagshaw
J. E. Lane

The Centre acknowledges with thanks the support provided by the Electronics and Avionics Requirements Board of the Department of Industry for the project from which this publication derives.

Introduction

Microcomputer networks provide a way of linking together microcomputers for the purpose of sharing such resources as information, communications, printing facilities, etc, within a department or over a complete site. The data transmission rates are typically less than 10 Mbps with a very low error rate.

Microcomputer (or personal computer) networks are available in a number of different topologies and utilising a number of different technologies. The main criterion is that the networks are relatively cheap to implement. The networks available range from dedicated networks with the main type of workstation designed for the office environment (but also providing interfaces for the more popular personal computers), to third party networks designed purely to interconnect specific personal computers and networks supplied by manufacturers for use solely with their proprietary equipment. The purpose of this book is to point out the problems and opportunities, should a network of personal computers be contemplated.

The book is meant to highlight some of the practical problems in planning, choosing and installing a personal computer network. Important points are summarised at the end of each relevant section. Continuous reference to these summaries should help in the avoidance of costly mistakes at an early stage in the planning process.

The first chapter puts the microcomputer network into perspective by considering other networks and looking at the history of data communications. The second chapter then looks at the applications to which these relatively new networks can be put and what this means to the end-user.

The third chapter covers requirements regarding hardware, software, installation, and management. The main aims are to explain what makes one type of personal computer more suitable for networking than another, the practical problems encountered, and the management required. Each section is summarised and can be used, as in other chapters, as a quick reference checklist for the user when talking to suppliers.

Chapters four and five cover the technologies available (and now encountered in suppliers' equipment) and the present standards situation. Chapter six considers the choice of a microcomputer network and the necessary stages involved in the selection process. Future developments are discussed in Chapter seven, and Appendix A provides a summary chart of various manufacturers' equipment.

Networking microcomputers opens up a whole new area of information to a greater number of end-users through communications. Just as cities sprang up as centres of commerce in the past, the reverse will be true in the future as improved communications removes the need for such large conurbations. The benefits of microcomputer networks for the small business user will be obvious as cheaper systems become available, while large businesses can use microcomputer networks as a basis for improved control on local cost centres, in addition to the improved communication and information access.

This book is intended for designers of computing and office systems who are looking at the implementation of microcomputer networks and assessing their potential. Individuals involved in traditional computing and telecommunications will also find the book useful in order to assess the impact of microcomputer networks on future corporate strategies by recognising their current capabilities and future potential.

Contents

	Page
Acknowledgements	
Introduction	
1 Networks	11
Introduction	11
The Definition of a Network	11
Wide Area Networks	17
Local Area Networks	22
Personal Computer Networks	24
Gateways	26
Bridges	27
The Impact of Networks	28
2 Applications	31
Introduction	31
Office Systems	31
Industrial Applications	40
Development Systems	41
Electronic Publishing	41
Education and Training	42
Community Services and Home Information	42
Medical Applications	42
CAD-CAM	43
Network Analysis	43

**3 Personal Computer Network
    Requirements**   45

    Introduction   45
    Hardware Requirements   45
    Software Requirements   69
    Installation Requirements   86
    Operational and Management Requirements   91

4 Technologies and Architectures Available   99

    Introduction   99
    Transmission Media   100
    Topologies   111
    Network Access and Sharing Methods   117

5 Standards   129

    Why the Need?   129
    Proprietary Architectures   130
    Open Systems Interconnection   131

6 Choosing a Microcomputer Network   141

    Introduction   141
    The Planning Stage   141
    The Specifying Stage   143
    The Tendering Stage   146
    The Installing Stage   146
    Conclusions   149

7 The Future   151

Appendix

  A Product Information   159
  B Glossary   165

References and Bibliography   181

Index   185

1 Networks

INTRODUCTION

Networks can be classified as falling under one of three main headings:

— wide area networks;

— local area networks;

— personal computer or microcomputer networks.

The local area network and the personal computer (or micro-computer) network are confined to a site or department. Providing that no external communication is required, involving wide area networks run by third parties, the network control is left completely in the hands of the end-user. Local area networks may incorporate the company's PABX as part of the overall plan. The emerging personal computer networks are concerned with connecting together personal computers (or microcomputers) in a cost-effective way. Because of how the price of personal computers has dropped over recent years the network used to link them must itself be relatively cheap to implement.

THE DEFINITION OF A NETWORK

A network cannot be defined concisely. It is more useful to classify it by the various components which interconnect and interact to provide, often remote, end-user to end-user communication. The network will have the following basic functions: transmission, switching and signalling (Figure 1.1).

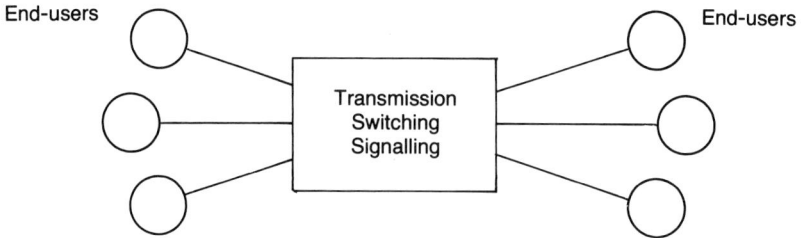

Figure 1.1   Network Functions

The network in common use providing end-user to end-user communication is the telephone network. It is totally invisible when used by individuals to set up voice communications on the network, providing they observe the conversation set-up protocols (ie lift the handset, wait for dial tone, dial the address or number, etc). However, it does provide the functions of transmission, switching and signalling. This network gives remote users the chance to communicate.

Figure 1.1 provides no explanation of where the network functions take place or how they are distributed, ie in the network itself or in the end-user terminals. In order to look at the possible distribution of these functions, consider first of all the telephone network.

The telephone network*, shown in Figure 1.2, is of a hierarchical design. This means that the basic design could be thought of in the form of a pyramid. The top of this pyramid, in the case of the telephone network, provides the International Gateway Exchange(s) which interconnects various countries (Figure 1.3).

At the base of the pyramid a large number of users will be connected to the network in order to take advantage of the facilities it provides. A structured approach such as this alleviates some of the problems encountered with transmission, switching

---

* The economic considerations for providing a large network are not examined in this book and the reader is directed to the references for this chapter. The general costing considerations for each layer of the network are important and are very relevant to the subject of this book.

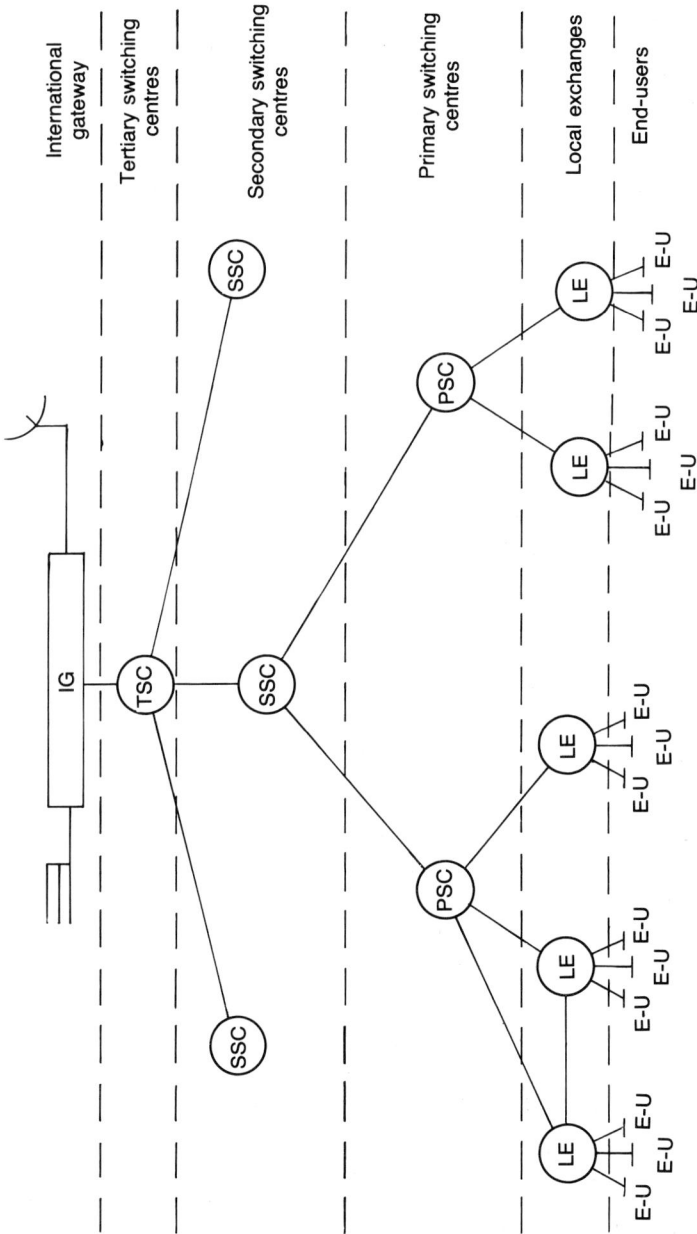

Figure 1.2   Hierarchical Design of the Public Switched Telephone Network

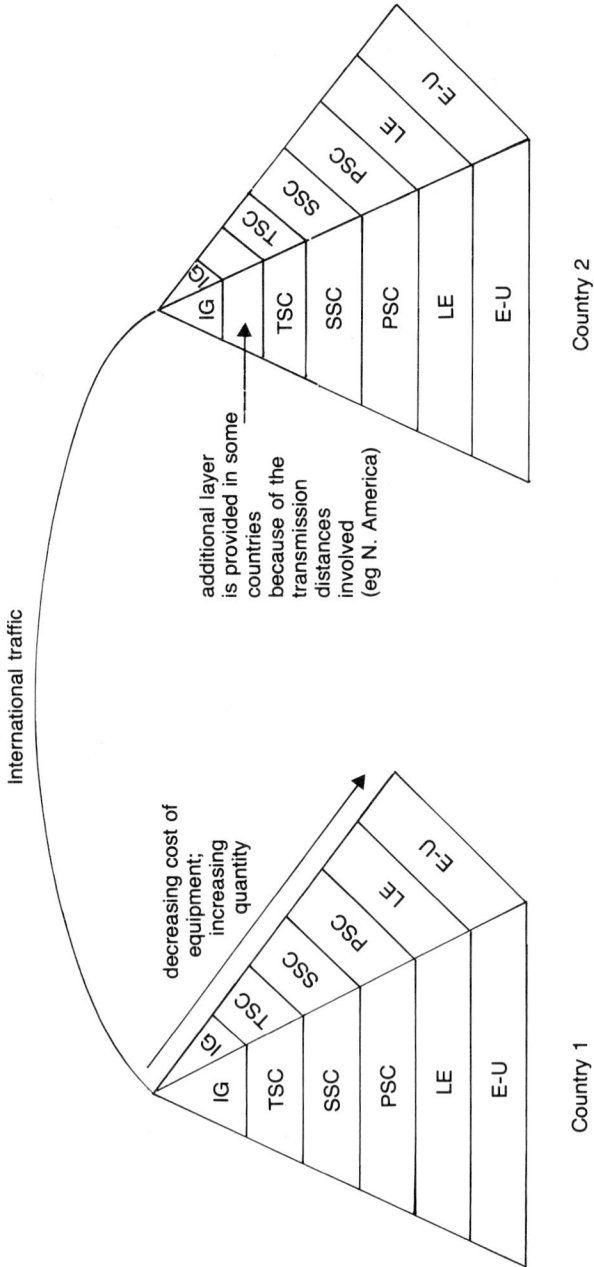

Figure 1.3   Pyramid Structure (Layers)

and signalling. Only a very small percentage of users will be using the international facilities at a given time and because the cost of providing international equipment is high (the equipment needs to be of a better quality in order to transmit over longer distances) it can be suitably dimensioned.

On the other hand, end-users at the base of the pyramid may only require local communications for the majority of cases so the transmission and terminal equipment may be of a low cost (lower quality because of the relatively short distances involved).

The pyramid structure thus provides a cost-effective solution to the geographical problems of providing a network where less of it is required.

An additional benefit of this type of structure is that all telephone exchanges at the Primary Switching Centre level, for example, can be slid out and replaced hence taking advantage of advances in technology. It is essential, of course, that the interfaces with the layer above it and the layer below it remain compatible.

In this type of system both star and mesh topologies, when the traffic demands a direct link (see Chapter 4), may co-exist.

The transmission function is provided both between levels and across levels. The switching function is provided at each level, even at the end-user level if for example a PABX (see Chapter 7) is employed. The signalling function is used to provide a cost-effective and efficient way of controlling the network.

The hierarchical nature of computer products may be thought of as falling into three basic categories:

— mainframe – used for number crunching;

— minicomputer – I/O transaction oriented;

— microcomputer – manipulative oriented (eg word processor).

In the future the end-user will probably see only two types of host-attached terminals:

— the very basic dumb terminals;

— the full capability microcomputer.

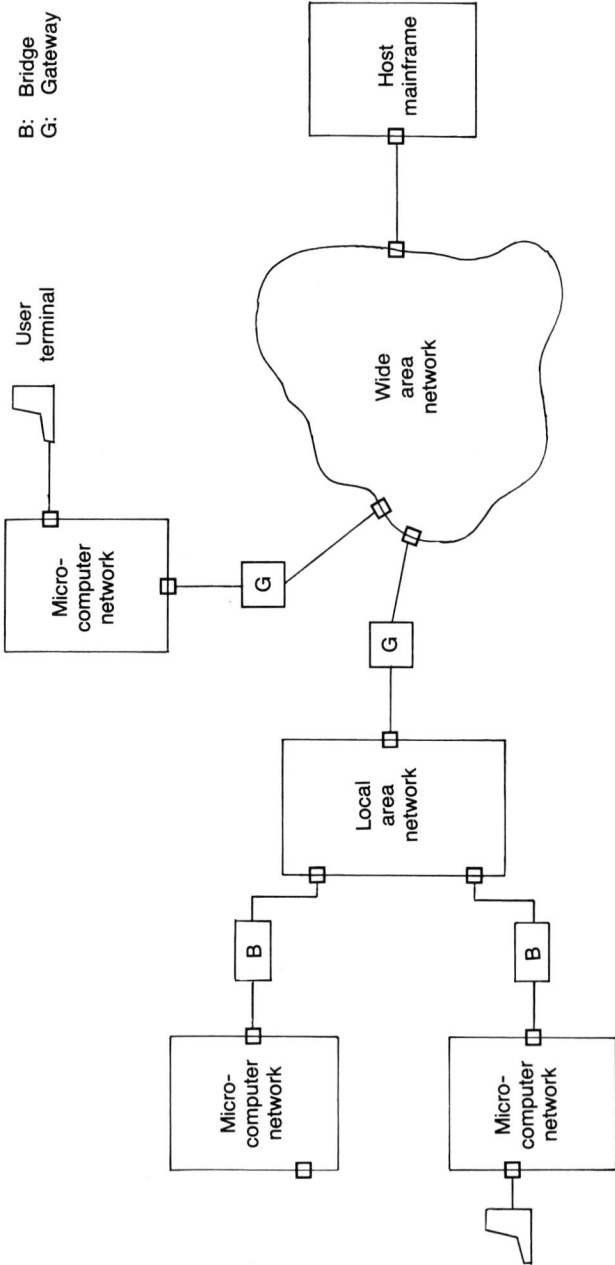

Figure 1.4   Possible Computer Network Configuration

All of the various products may require interconnection, preferably over some sort of network.

If, for example, there was a requirement for a database, held on the mainframe, to be downloaded to a microcomputer (or microcomputers) for manipulation then the microcomputer(s) may well be given access to the mainframe by clustering them on an intermediate minicomputer into which the database would be loaded.

The configuration of a computer network could well take the form shown in Figure 1.4.

The local area network could include a PABX. This aspect, along with wide area networks, microcomputer (or personal computer) networks, gateways and bridges will be discussed in the following sections of this chapter.

The final section considers the impact of networks. It must be noted that integrated networks are being designed today to support a diverse range of communications:

— voice;

— video;

— data;

— text.

New microcomputer-based devices are becoming available to support a number of these communications activities.

WIDE AREA NETWORKS

The geographical area of a wide area network is much wider than that of a local area network.

To put networks into perspective: the microcomputer network may be used within an individual department in a company; the local area network will be confined to one site within the company; and the wide area network is used whenever the communications leaves that site in the form of electrical signals on a cable, or using a satellite, providing it involves a third party, eg PTT.

Wide area network systems are rarely offered as commercial

products in the way that local area networks are. They are offered as services to the end-user who wants to interconnect several remotely located sites to a control computer facility or interconnect several local area networks.

The data transmitted over a wide area network could utilise a number of different types of transmission media including telephone lines, land lines, coax cables, radio satellite and optical fibre links. In addition the wide area network may be classified as transmitting only selected data types or a wide range of types as specified by the integrated networks described in the preceding section.

Wide area networks can most usefully be described as those using telephone systems and lines and those using specially designed data networks. The data networks can then be subdivided into those using circuit switching, message switching or packet switching.

These services are usually provided by public authorities; however, in the UK, because of liberalisation and the privatisation of BT, they are now provided by licensed companies. These companies are generally called PTTs (Postal, Telegraph and Telephone Authorities).

The Public Switched Telephone Network

During a normal telephone conversation the circuit is established for the duration of the call. This circuit is purely temporary and is established over the PSTN. Once the call is finished, the devices are disconnected and the circuit is dropped.

Data communications originally used the PSTN to connect computers to remote terminals. At the present time PRESTEL uses telephone lines to link users' terminals with the database computers. Many personal computer networks provide interfaces in order to access other network users.

The PSTN, however, was never designed to transmit data. The telephone network itself is analogue and in order to connect a piece of digital equipment to the line it is necessary either to use a modem (modulator-demodulator) to translate the signals from digital to analogue and back again, or an acoustic coupler which changes the digital signal into sound patterns that are fed into the telephone microphone and decoded at the telephone receiver.

Many large companies use leased circuits or leased lines. These provide the user with the ability to transmit higher data rates because they are selected to be in a low noise environment and directly patched across the switching equipment at the exchange. Usually a telephone connection limits the bandwidth of a channel to 3400 Hz. However, it is possible to lease a number of these multiplexed channels in order to provide a wider bandwidth. For example, leasing 12 circuits provides 48 KHz while leasing 60 circuits provides 240 KHz. The names given to the translating processes in building up the hierarchies are those of the hierarchy being translated. This means that the modulation process which builds from groups into supergroups is called group translating. The CCITT multiplex hierarchy is shown in Table 1.1.

Name	Number of Channels	Bandwidth (KHz)
1 channel	1	3.1
2 group	12	48
3 supergroup	60	240
4 mastergroup	300	1232
5 super mastergroup	900	3872
6 12 MHz system	2700	12062

(The BT and North American hierarchies have their own variations on the above for points 4, 5 and 6.)

Table 1.1   CCITT Multiplex Hierarchy

Standard channel spacing for frequency division multiplexing is 4000 Hz (not 3400 Hz), so as to provide a guard band in order to minimise the effects of cross-talk from other channels (see Chapter 4), for channels up to the supergroup level.

Data Networks

Public switched and private leased data networks have their advantages and disadvantages. The former can offer circuit or packet switching together with the economics and, for the user, the potential for a wider range of access to other users than a private network can offer, although this does depend upon the implementation of agreed protocols and standards (see Chapter 5). Private networks, however, have the ability to respond much more quickly to a company's requirements and to provide a more tailored solution. They can be more expensive, depending upon the use to which they are put.

Public networks are meant to satisfy the needs of the majority of users while private networks can provide more exact solutions for the individual.

Circuit Switched Data Networks

In this form each computer has a private circuit to a local exchange and it is the exchanges themselves that form a wide area network. A path is found through the network each time that communication needs to be established between a pair of given devices. A control system, usually separate from the data network, is used to send messages which establish the circuits as and when required.

The disadvantages of this type of network come about because the circuits are not always reliable enough for computer communications. The circuit can only be used by the two computers while the call is set up and a call can take several seconds to set up. The advantages are that it is favourable to those end-users requiring calls to be set up for a short time and could be used when a single device is communicating for long periods of time.

Interestingly enough, circuit switching will be used for data transmission with the installation and subsequent use of System X exchanges (see Chapter 7).

Message Switched Data Networks

This type of network may also be described as a store-and-forward technique. The devices on the network exchange information by sending each other messages. These messages will then be stored at intermediate nodes in the network and forwarded when possible. The user devices do not have to wait for a connection, however, because of the store-and-forward method there could be some delay before the message reaches its final destination.

Message switched networks are those used for telegraph and telex.

It is possible, with both circuit and message switching, that congestion may occur in the network under heavy loading.

When congestion does occur there can be a very long delay before a call path can be set up to an end-user.

Congestion in message switched networks may well occur because the intermediate nodes in the network have run out of buffers in which to store an incoming message, while in circuit switched networks congestion may occur because of blocking in the network switch or switches.

Packet Switched Networks

This type of network follows on as a development of message switched networks, described above. Here the messages are broken up into packets which have a maximum length, pre-defined by the network. It is the packets that are then transmitted across the network. Clearly because the message is broken up into packets and there is a possibility that one packet may get lost resulting in a wrong message being delivered, there must be some sort of control. Each packet has a header which includes the destination and a number of data bytes, followed by the actual data and completed with a tail containing checking information (ie a cyclic redundancy check).

As you have probably already noticed this type of network is a little more complex than the ordinary message switched network from which it evolved. It does have a number of advantages including the fact that very long messages can be broken up into manageable packets. In order to take advantage of these manageable packet sizes it is essential that a packet network provides the following facilities:

— buffering of packets at nodes;

— control of errors;

— packet routeing;

— flow and congestion control.

LOCAL AREA NETWORKS

This type of network is usually centred on a small site such as an office block, factory or university campus. The network, in order to achieve a designation of local, will not come under the control of any external PTT simply because it does not use any of the facilities provided by the PTT.

Local area networks evolved by getting caught between a number of converging techniques and technologies, namely computer networks (the type discussed in the wide area network section) on the one hand, and microprocessors and Very Large Scale Integration (VLSI) of chip sets on the other. Although the original requirement was for computers to communicate (Gee, 1982), the development has gone far beyond this.

While wide area networks have typical data transmission rates in the order of 100s to 1000s of bits per second with a maximum of about 50,000, transmitted from about 1 km to 100 km and upwards, local area networks range from 10 to 100 million bits per second at typical distances of between 1 and 10 km.

Local area networks are essentially meant as a method of connecting a large number of computer-based devices on a single site. In order to achieve this interconnection in a cost-effective and productive way the local area network must have the following features built into the design:

— inexpensive transmission media (in many but not all instances);

— inexpensive devices to attach to the media;

— ease of device connection to the media;

— high data transmission rates (with low error rates);

— network transmission rate to be independent of attached device transmission rate;

— interconnection between devices (resource sharing);

— intercommunication between devices.

The above points will be expanded in later chapters.

A local area network can provide the potential to share files or printer resources. For the moment the local area network will be described as having the modular components shown in Figure 1.5.

The modules shown are by no means exhaustive. Individual suppliers will provide varying numbers of these modules, although suppliers of complete systems will provide the file servers, print servers, etc.

It is important to note that local area network suppliers do not provide fully open systems. At worst they are completely closed to the particular vendor's products and at best they are only partially open.

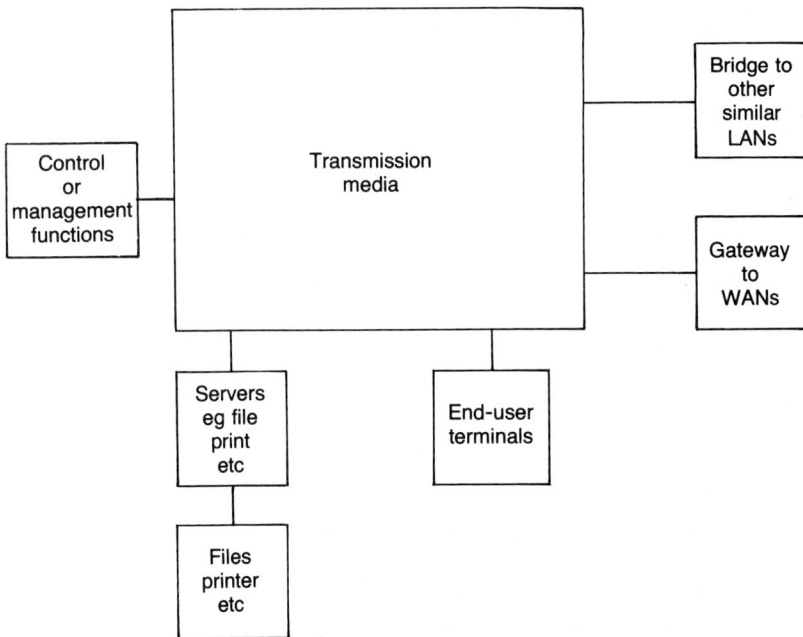

Figure 1.5   Modular Presentation of a LAN

This has become even more of an issue when considering personal computer networks or micro-networks.

PERSONAL COMPUTER NETWORKS

Local area networks, providing the integration for many data types, will in general have data rates running from 10M bits per second to 100M bits per second.

Personal computer networks on the other hand generally have data rates below 10M bits per second – because of cost and the applications to which these networks are put. These two reasons (cost and applications) will not remain in the same form in the future but their use in arguments for network justification will undoubtedly remain.

To clarify this point we will consider high data rate networks. These networks use high bandwidth and at the moment high-cost cables. This type of network is hard to justify for use with cheap personal computers which are readily available, off the shelf, requiring only an interface card (if one is available for the particular network) to be inserted into the peripheral slot of the personal computer, along with some software, in order to provide a network connection.

The same argument that was used for the cable (ie cost) applies to the interface cards. The cost of providing an interface card to the network may well approach the cost of the personal computer itself, making its networking less attractive.

Next we must turn to the applications. Personal computers were never built with networking in mind, although this situation is now changing with some of the newer products on the market – but not *all* of the newer products.

The problem of networking a personal computer comes about because of the basic architecture of the design. The microcomputer market grew up using 8-bit processors, consequently a large amount of 8-bit software has been developed and is in use. The advent of 16-bit (and latterly 32-bit) processors has presented the industry with a problem: how to sell 16-bit hardware considering the investment in 8-bit software.

One way of overcoming this problem is to put an 8-bit processor and a 16-bit processor in the same environment and write an operating system to decide which one should be used. A number of companies have opted for this dual-processor solution.

Personal computers used in a network configuration require a different architecture to those used in a stand-alone environment. The attention now is drawn towards a co-processor approach for personal computer architectures with special chips being designed in for specific purposes (eg memory management, I/O transactions, arithmetic functions, logical functions, etc).

The personal computer network does provide the small business with access to shared resources and the large business, in addition to this, the chance to control individual departments much more closely as regional cost centres, not to mention improving the communications. The benefit of a personal computer network is that it provides a relatively cheap network within the price range of many small businesses and within the budget of many departments.

In order to gain the maximum use of a personal computer network, its strengths and weaknesses (discussed later in the book) must be fully understood. No two networks are exactly the same. Choosing a network for personal computers is usually approached in one of two ways:

(1)   I already have some personal computers and can now see a requirement to network them (eg resource sharing), or

(2)   I can see a requirement for a personal computer network (eg to improve efficiency). The complete network is to be installed from day one.

In some ways approach (1) is easier, simply because there will probably be fewer options. However, it could make the interworking of networks very difficult. Approach (2) provides the opportunity to design the network from a 'clean sheet'. However, requirements and uses must be well defined.

Points to stress are: from the first approach above – just because your business or company has personal computers it does not

necessarily mean that they can be networked easily and economi-
cally on a personal computer network.

From the second approach – the requirements and uses must be
clearly defined as it is likely that computers will be used in the
environment for the first time.

GATEWAYS

A gateway provides a local area network or personal computer
network with the ability to gain access to a wide area network. The
gateway opens the door for communication to external devices,
external computers and external services.

The gateway itself provides an interface between two networks
which have incompatible higher-level protocols. In view of the
large number of network options, and the basic incompatibilities
between them, a general-purpose gateway would have to be an
enormously flexible and powerful machine. Most suppliers of networks will develop gateways to external devices, computers and
services as the market demands.

A gateway allows a number of users to gain access to the external
function. In addition to the communications interfaces provided
on both sides, the gateway could also have any one or more of the
following characteristics:

— protocol conversion;

— circuit switching;

— contention;

— store and forward (buffering);

— route selection (addressing);

— network control (time-outs, error recovery);

— network management (including accounting and statistics);

— access control (including security).

The acceptance of standards will help the widespread use of
gateways by reducing the large number of possible interfaces and
encouraging users and suppliers to develop and implement local

area networks and hence gateways. The long-term outlook must be to create a single gateway in order to access the Integrated Services Digital Network (ISDN) that will come about with the installation of System X telephone exchanges.

The gateway not only looks at each packet on the first network but also modifies the content or format so as to be able to present it to the second network in a way that is acceptable (see Figure 1.6).

The gateway provides a function up to layer 3 of the ISO reference model (see Chapter 5).

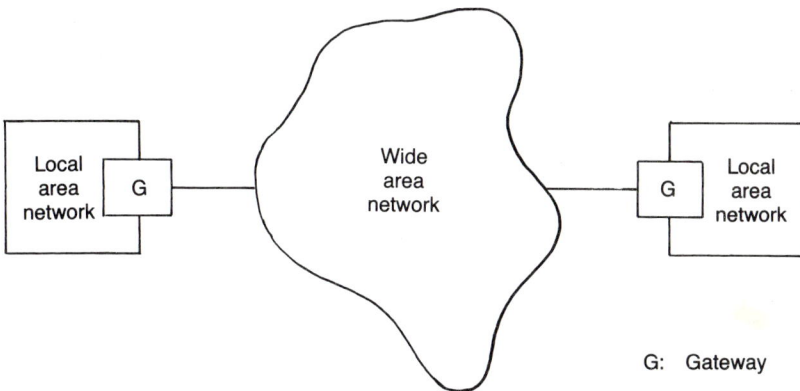

G: Gateway

Figure 1.6   Gateway Function

BRIDGES

Bridges provide a function by which two similar local area net-works are able to function and act as one (Figure 1.7). Packets on the network are read by the bridge but no modification is made to the content or format: none is required because both networks use the same protocols.

The bridge provides a function up to layer 2 of the ISO reference model (see Chapter 5). Bridges can be very useful in reconfiguring a network design in order to take account of reliability, perfor-mance, security or simply convenience.

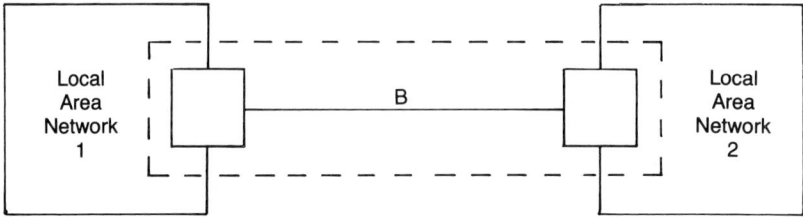

B: Bridge

LAN 1 and LAN 2 are *similar* local area networks

Figure 1.7   Bridge Function

THE IMPACT OF NETWORKS

This section provides some thoughts and stimulates ideas concerning the effect of the networks discussed in our everyday lives. (The reader's attention is directed towards the references for this chapter for more detailed information.)

The justification of a network or the connection to external network services needs to be based on a careful analysis of both costs and benefits. Many of the costs of running an office are unlikely to be reduced much by applying information technology. Typical breakdowns for the distribution of office costs are:

— face-to-face communications   25%;

— analysis and decision   21%;

— telephone   20%;

— preparation of letters and reports   15%;

— moving paper   12%;

— typing   4%;

— copying   3%;

Some of the gains achieved through information technology, although appearing marginal, could still be very worthwhile. The cost of skilled labour is beginning to rise while the cost of hardware, and in some instances software, is falling.

Network	Typical	Advantages	Disadvantages	Comments
Wide Area Network	transmitting data over geographically large distances	usually run by a PTT or private company; no need to worry about maintaining a large network privately; gives a wider access to remote users; flexible; provides remote resource sharing (corporate)	some do not provide adequate network management (for the end user); low transmission rates (relative to LAN); high probability of errors in transmitted data (relative to LAN)	specialised data networks may be used using complicated protocols; the advent of ISDN (see Chapter 7) will solve many of the problems; the switch must encompass flexibility and must be non-blocking
Local Area Network	transmitting data within a site, building, or university campus	higher data rates; self-contained and hence managed; third-party network suppliers are available to support other supplier's equipment; provide local resource sharing (divisional); low probability of errors	expansion can be a problem; many are 'closed' systems to a particular supplier's equipment; even third-party network suppliers do not provide 'open' systems	the networks must tend towards the structure of the OSI model; in the future gateways should also provide the 'open' connection to the WAN
Personal Computer (or micro-computer) Network	transmitting data within a department	cheap networking facilities; high data rates (but lower than LANs); shared resources with the subsequent possible benefits; self-contained – self-managed	most are 'closed' systems; most personal computers were not built with networking in mind; care must be taken concerning the personal computer's power to perform certain tasks; no standard systems	the area is evolving; the critical areas are hardware (architecture of personal computer to be used on a network) and software (operating systems used)

Figure 1.8 Network Summary

Networks provide the opportunity to communicate and share resources. The resources may not involve merely sharing local files and printers but may also comprise network services usually described as value-added services.

The networks described in this chapter allow the user to access an increasing amount of information. However, much will depend on various specific circumstances when considering installation and usage. Existing staff may be trained to operate the equipment effectively. The network may provide not only the opportunity to use value-added networks but also the chance to create value-added staff! It is worthwhile to summarise some of the points highlighted in the various networks (Figure 1.8).

2 Applications

INTRODUCTION

This chapter investigates the applications to which a network may be put. We will see (in Appendix A) that certain networks perform particular tasks very well indeed: they were designed to perform the function right from the start. This does not mean that a system which is good at one task will not be good at another, but that the applications should not be too diverse. In fact there are many specific functions for which networks can be used, ranging from dedicated office systems to dedicated engineering systems. The important point is that if a compromise system is chosen to perform more than one task, the end-users needs must be met.

OFFICE SYSTEMS

The normal tasks performed in an office can easily be carried out on an office network system. These tasks will include the following:

Text or Report Preparation (Word Processing)

This involves typing, updating and correcting the material. It may be implemented by presenting a typist at a workstation with a hand-written or dictated draft version which could then be entered into the system. The typed version may then be viewed, read and corrected at the originator's terminal so as to verify the final copy before giving the go-ahead for distribution.

Message Distribution

Making telephone calls is a problem where people are never available. Message distribution allows internal electronic mail or memos to be sent to specific persons. Increasingly, the terminals of the newer systems provide the facility to send a voice message. The voice is digitised, sent to the target terminal, and retrieved by the targetted user. The benefit of this is that any urgency in the message, which may be otherwise lost in a hand-written version, is fully understood from the tone of the voice. Message distribution does not just mean sending out messages, but can also take on another form. For example, it is sometimes possible to make up, from a dictionary of set words on the system, an appropriate voice message to act as an automatic answering service.

Personal Information Management

This involves the use of software functions that mimic the parts of the office that we have all become familiar with. These include filing cabinets, in/out trays, diaries and planning charts (eg spreadsheets).

Non-Personal Information Access

This allows access to reference documents, library, other system users' information (shared access of files), corporate information and external databases. Non-personal information access will at some time or other require the user to go outside the immediate network. This external access may be to an adjoining network via a bridge or external database, using the public network, via a gateway, or via a modem.

Electronic office systems are merely tools which help the office worker to perform everyday tasks. They must be simple to operate and tolerant of a user's mistakes. Attention should be given to:

— *the workstation:* in order to access and use the file and services provided it must:

— be easy to use;

— have local processing power;

— provide access to printer and personal file storage;

— be designed for office rather than scientific use.

— *shared facilities:* these should include:

    — a letter quality printer;

    — a good quality printer;

    — data processing access;

    — disk storage;

    — service program;

    — archiving.

— *access to external facilities:*

    — databases;

    — information services;

    — data networks;

    — electronic mail services (telex and teletex);

    — facsimile.

— *communications:*

    — to link the workstation to services;

    — to inter-link workstations;

    — to provide access to shared facilities;

    — to provide ease of use.

The facilities of an office system should be provided as part of the network rather than as separate add-ons. The system operation should remain, for the most part, transparent to the user. At the same time it is necessary to have access to traffic statistics in order to monitor the network performance. The difference between a word processing system and an electronic office system can be seen by comparing Figure 2.1 and Figure 2.2.

Information Management System

Information is a resource. Information management is concerned with accessing and using the resource to the benefit of the company. The information held by a company can be on a corporate or

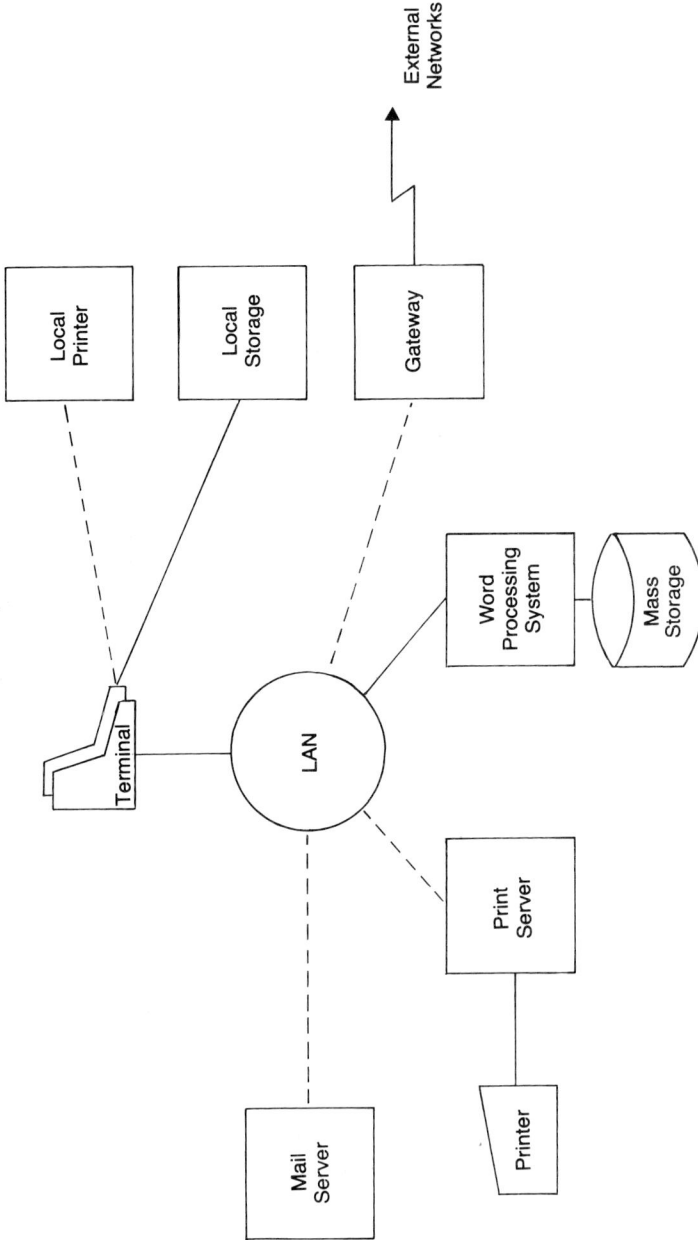

Figure 2.1   Word Processing System

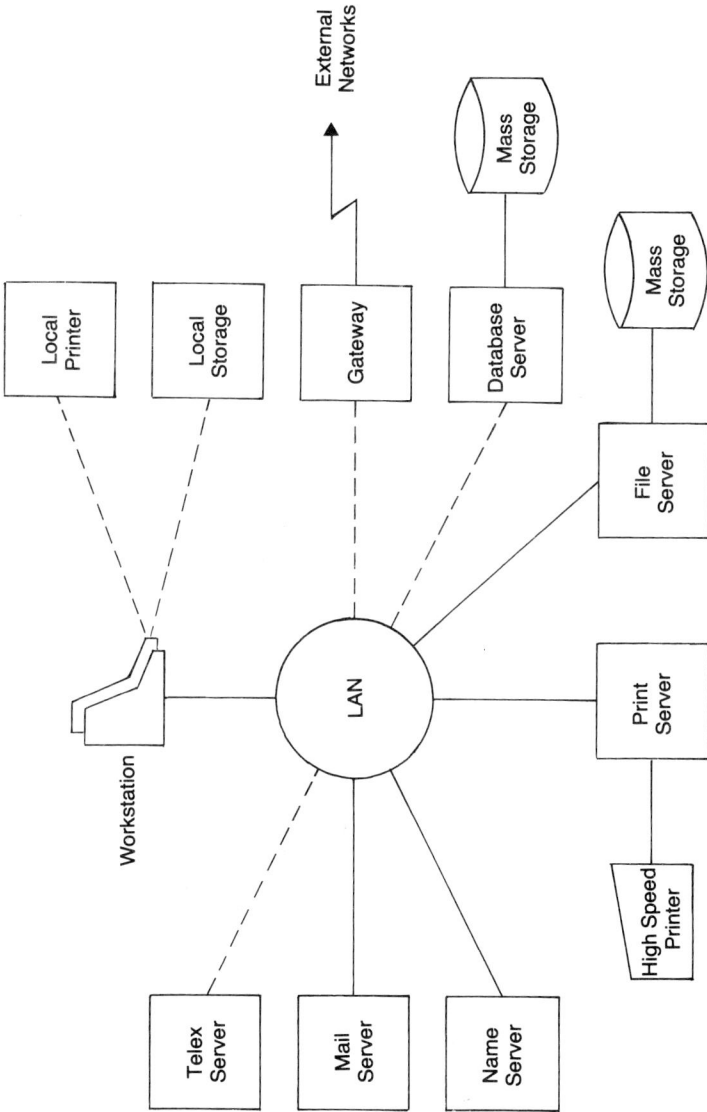

Figure 2.2   Electronic Office System

personal level. The corporate information will reside on a central, usually a mainframe, system while the personal information will reside on a local system, either a workstation with floppy disks or a workstation attached to a local network.

The corporate information will include data on such things as the trading performance of the organisation as a whole, and provides that information to help the running of the company. The personal information will provide the individual with the data required to make the organisation of his own work easier, eg telephone numbers, diaries, names and addresses, details of meetings, etc.

Some companies use the workstation as an effective tool to access both corporate and personal information. In such circumstances, precautions must be taken to protect confidential information from unauthorised access. Personal computer networks are becoming increasingly useful in accessing external databases, or corporate information.

The corporate information resident on the company's mainframe may be accessed using a terminal emulator and a suitable gateway. In this way a number of terminals on a network may gain shared access to the company's mainframe. This automatic access via the gateway devices makes the overall system much more flexible. This flexibility is reflected in the possibility of accessing external, third-party databases which may be specialist science and business information, bibliographic data, patents files or the more general information services such as Prestel.

Not all personal computer networks have gateways (or bridges, for that matter) available as extras. It is essential therefore that should access to external information be required, either at present or in the future, that the requirements are included at the design stage.

The convergence of office technology, computer science, information science and telecommunications will call for the role of an information manager (Horton, 1979). The information manager will exist on a corporate and departmental level. Whether, at the corporate level, the manager is born out of the data processing department is not under consideration.

It is essential however that he should coordinate the evolution of the personal computer network, considering its potential use as an information tool. Whether the organisation is large or small, the role of the information manager remains the same. The responsibilities of the information manager, or anyone involved in choosing a personal computer network to be used for information management, are to:

— coordinate the planning, development and operation of corporate and departmental information systems;

— develop policies and technical guidance to assist in the management of information systems;

— improve systems compatibility through the promotion of standards of hardware and software;

— establish and operate a company information centre, which will maintain an inventory of the information – data as well as software – contained on other systems;

— provide training programs;

— provide technical advice, possibly also a 'hot-line' service;

— provide short-term and long-term plans covering information needs of both the company and the individuals.

Electronic Message System

An electronic message system is used to transfer messages between a group of users. In order that it should work effectively, a minimum amount of equipment is required as follows:

— a central filing system in order to store the messages;

— a workstation for each user in the group;

— full interconnectability between the workstations and the message handling system.

The electronic message system should then provide the following facilities:

— to write and edit messages;

— to direct messages to one person or to broadcast them;

— to provide confirmation of delivery;
— to store a received message;
— to reply to a received message;
— to provide message privacy.

In addition to these facilities the workstation itself must provide a user-friendly interface. This may take the form of a flag appearing on the screen, or other type of visual aid, whenever incoming mail is received. This in itself will make the use of the system much easier as constantly checking the workstation for the arrival of new mail is no longer required. A priority flag may also be set.

The electronic message system for personal computer networks will typically use the keyboard as user interface. There are however, some workstations that provide a voice messaging system. They are usually employed in conjunction with the newer computerised telephone exchanges and hence form a star network. Some have a local area network attachment. Using a local area network to attach the workstations does usually provide ease of system expansion and is relatively inexpensive.

The messaging system itself may assume an active or passive role. Systems used for an active role provide the basis of a telephone answering system. A dictionary of key words provided with the system software may be used to build a message in order to provide a set answer to be used for incoming calls. For example, if the message system interacts with the user's personal diary and the system's real-time clock, then a message could be set up to answer any enquiries made to that workstation during lunchtimes, meetings, holidays, etc.

The passive role, explained previously, takes place when the workstation acknowledges and flags up any incoming messages but no attempt is made by the system to immediately offer an answer. Both active and passive systems may use voice and/or text for communicating the message.

The principles of the electronic message system are extended into the educational requirements of a network. In this case a master workstation may be used to directly interrogate and copy over the slave workstation's screen onto the master. However, the system in this case is merely providing a utility allowing the message to be fed directly to the end-user, usually to provide guidance.

When dealing with electronic message systems for personal computers, one must not develop an inward-looking attitude. Once again the question of the availability of suitable gateways arises. The network must be equipped with a gateway device for the public system in order to use such facilities as BT Gold.

Database Access

Accessing a database and searching for information is performed in one of two ways. *Searches* may use keys and other methods of enquiry and is one such approach used for information retrieval (loosely structured). Alternatively, in the *database* approach the information is organised in a more systematic way (tightly structured). The records contained within the database have fixed formats which have fixed numbers of fields of fixed sizes.

The enquiries are usually clearly defined with set rules for answering them. The difference must be pointed out between a file and a database. A file will comprise a set of records to be used for one particular application.

A database will comprise a collection of interrelated application-independent data. This does not mean that because databases are structured they are also rigid. In fact the whole database, or records within it, may be updated at any time. This leads to the problem of multiple updating of the individual records and also to the problem of record locking, a difficulty shared with file locking and causing the attempted simultaneous update of a record or file (see Chapter 3). Many personal computer networks do not provide this facility. At best it is provided at the partition level and at worse must be written into the applications software. The access is usually allowed but the attempted multiple update only becomes evident when a 'write' is performed.

Personal computer networks offer the facility to download a copy of the database to the user workstation where it may be modified or incorporated into local applications programs. The integration of the database, or relevant parts of the database, with the end-user's data will result in much more up-to-date information being available at the remote workstation. It is of course absolutely essential that the configuration of the source data in the database is such that it is in a suitable format to be used in the application package which is running in the end-user's workstation. The personal computer that provides local processing is very useful in these applications.

Clearly the ease of use of personal computers and personal computer networks in this and other types of application can very easily lead to an ease of misuse. Careful control must be exercised whenever common data is used for a number of applications.

Networks then will also lend themselves to distributed database systems where users on the network have access to databases on another similar network. The networks in this instance may be linked by a bridge. As we will see later (Chapter 3) a bridge used in this way could form the basis of a security structure. The consideration of using a distributed database system requires the user to address the following points:

— *cost:* the effect of distributing the data on the users and suppliers;

— *reliability:* the effect of distributing the data on its access;

— *security:* the effect of distributing the data on unauthorised access.

The possible requirement to access VIDEOTEX and VIEWDATA, and hence the availability of relevant gateways, must also be considered.

INDUSTRIAL APPLICATIONS

Networks are in use in manufacturing and on the factory floor for communications purposes. However, more demanding applications lie in the area of real-time industrial control systems.

Within the automatic test equipment environment the IEEE bus (see Chapter 3) has been used for many years in order to ensure that a range of electronic equipment (eg digital voltmeters, counter/timers, etc) could gain access to a unit-under-test.

When considering personal computer networks for use as real-time control systems their performance must come under scrunity. The performance of the system may severely degrade under loading, resulting in an increased response time. This is not a desirable aspect of a real-time system unless the load curve is known and the system designed to work well within the limits of the network performance. In this respect a deterministic rather than a probabalistic technique for network access will govern the choice of the system.

The question of providing redundant or stand-by equipment also arises. Should the master system be unavailable for any reason then the system chosen must provide an adequate slave back-up.

DEVELOPMENT SYSTEMS

Networks for use in this category of applications fall into two sections:

— personal computer networks on which the software may be developed for the final use on a larger mainframe system. These are proprietary systems available for software development and electronic office systems;

— a microprocessor development system on which the software is developed for specific microprocessor target boards. The system is used exclusively for engineering development with none of the flexibility of typical personal computer networks.

ELECTRONIC PUBLISHING

The electronic publishing application involves a number of ways of applying computing, electronics and information technology to the dissemination of information. This type of information would previously have been distributed on paper using normal printing techniques. The whole area of electronic publishing may include such areas as the automatic generation of viewdata frames from information already stored in a computer system, videotex news service, word processing, and computer typesetting. Electronic publishers may use word processors at workstations in order to enter and edit data, access databases and information systems, and then modify and correct text so that it is in the form ready for typesetting. There is a possibility in the future that the publishers themselves become more and more involved in the area of supplying information in the form of on-line databases. The commodity sold will still be information but the method of distribution will be different.

EDUCATION AND TRAINING

A number of suppliers have networks suitable for use in the field of education.

The mere fact that networks, with suitable facilities, provide access to a greater amount of information enhances their use for educational purposes. It also provides early experience of computing techniques. With the advent of optical disk storage there is even more emphasis being placed on interactive teaching and training. Videotex and viewdata systems devote a number of pages to education and some systems will support software that will allow the capture and manipulation of these frames. A personal computer network can provide the introduction of information technology into education, concerning itself with:

— communication;

— information retrieval;

— information handling.

COMMUNITY SERVICES AND HOME INFORMATION

Community information services have already been developed and are available through the videotex and viewdata services. The cheaper networks could be used to link homes in a particular neighbourhood or area. A community watch system is already in operation. It is not based on an off-the-shelf personal computer network, but could very easily be adapted to incorporate one where circumstances permit (McLuckie, 1984). Personal computers linked to local networks provide a vast opportunity in terms of home applications.

MEDICAL APPLICATIONS

Networks may be used most usefully in the area of on-line information retrieval. The possibility of accessing the medical records of a patient from remote locations is becoming increasingly realistic. The standardisation of patients' records will greatly enhance the use of computer systems for medical applications while the networking of computer systems will provide better access to the records. One problem is that systems for storing medical records have strict security requirements. The requirements of privacy, security and data management must be met not merely by a single database but by the network itself.

The medical applications also spill over into the area of community services and touch on the methods of entering data into the end-user terminal. Patients unable to operate a keyboard could use touch, sound or even voice recognition units.

CAD-CAM

The industrial applications of a network include process control, computer-aided design, and computer-aided manufacture.

It has long been the ambition of industry to support and integrate design and development information, manufacturing information and testing information on a single network. The benefits gained from a centralised information structure are typically the non-duplication of data from the initial design stage through prototyping and on to full-scale manufacture.

CAD-CAM has been available for many years but is only now coming into use on personal computer networks. Micro-based CAD systems must have features such as parameterisations, symbols, multiple layering and other data management facilities for engineering libraries, in common with their mini and mainframe counterparts. These features are now beginning to emerge. The benefit of using a personal computer network for CAD-CAM applications is that it can be employed also for other purposes and is not simply a dedicated engineering tool. In this respect the justification of a system is much easier, because it is more cost-effective.

NETWORK ANALYSIS

This relates not to the actual operation of the network itself but the use of Project Evaluation and Review Technique (PERT) and Critical Path Analysis (CPA) for project planning and control. Although, these methods can be run on a stand-alone personal computer, the benefits of employing them on a network of personal computers arise from the chance to access and use up-to-date data for the actual project analysis. Where projects rely on many interdependent activities from a number of departments, a network is used to correlate the data and identify at a very early stage in a project which activity is going wrong.

The applications discussed in this chapter cover a very broad range. Not every supplier can provide equipment from his product range that is suitable for every application. This means that the applications, both present and future, for which the personal computer network will be used must be carefully thought out at the design stage. It may be expensive or impossible to adapt a personal computer network beyond its original design.

3 Personal Computer Network Requirements

INTRODUCTION

The network requirements are discussed under four heads:

— hardware;

— software;

— installation;

— operational and management.

Although these requirements are discussed separately, their interaction is important. For a user to be able to discuss his own network requirements, he should not think of each type of requirement in isolation.

HARDWARE REQUIREMENTS

The network's hardware requirements are examined by looking at: the hardware required for local interworking, and the hardware required for wide interworking. The various parts of a personal computer network are shown in Figure 3.1.

This section concentrates mainly on the hardware for the personal computer. This consists of the important aspects of the personal computer architecture, including the subsystems such as memory (important to run the application's software) and input and output (important for communications). A network provides not only the ability to share resources but also the opportunity for improved communications.

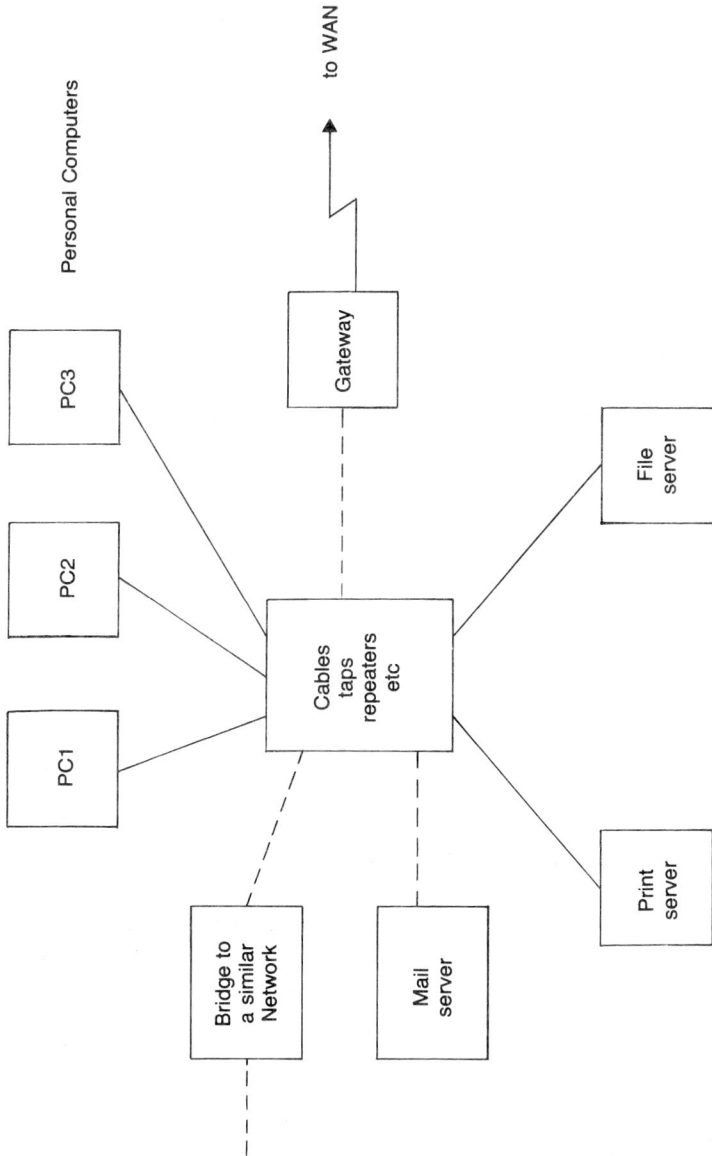

Figure 3.1 Personal Computer Network

Local Requirements

The main constituent parts of a computer comprise:

— clock;

— central processor unit (cpu);

— memory;

— input;

— output.

These parts together comprise the architecture of the hardware. They determine the power of the personal computer to perform certain tasks when it is connected into a network configuration. The microprocessor (the cpu) used in the personal computer has an immediate impact on a number of important areas. These include:

— classification by number of bits;

— instructions (how many are available);

— input/output word size;

— direct addressing;

— direct memory addressing.

More details of these and other features of some of the popular microprocessors may be found by referring to Figure 3.2. The ability to understand the relevance of these features, explored in this section, helps the user to assess the suitability of a personal computer for a network (from the point of view of performance), and to assess the suitability of an applications program for use on a particular personal computer. The overall performance of a network – in terms of response times and availability – is greatly affected by not just the applications software, operating system software and network capacity but also the architecture of the terminal and peripheral equipment. For example, if the input and output sections are not designed correctly then no amount of elegantly written software can correct the situation. This should be taken into account when assessing personal computers for use in a network environment.

If the network is to link together several personal computers

MICROPROCESSOR FEATURE	Z80	6502	8088	8086	Z8000	MC68000	HP FOCUS
Classification by bits	8	8	8/16	16	16	16/32	32
Internal architecture (bits)	8	8	16	16	16	32	32
Power dissipation (watts)	1	.575	1.5	1.5	.8	1.2	7
Clock frequency (MHz)	2.5	1/2	5	5/8/10	4/6/10	6/8/12.5	18
Data bus (bits)	8	8	8	16	16	16	32
Data word size (bits)	8	8	8-16	8-16	1/4/8/16/32/64	16	32-64
Instruction word size (bits)	8	8	8-48	8-48	16/32/48	16	38
Input/output word size (bits)	8	8	8	8/16	8/16	8/16/32	32
Direct addressing capability (bytes)	256	256	64K	64K	64K	16M	500M
Direct memory addressing	standard	no	optional	optional	standard	optional	standard
Instructions	158	56	134	134	110	56	230
Registers (arithmetic/index/general-purpose)	14/2/6	1/2/2	0/0/8	0/0/8	0/0/16	8/16/16	7/10/11

Figure 3.2   Microprocessor Features

already in use then the operational limitations of the networked personal computers must be understood. The limitations may take the form of the personal computer being 'under powered' if used as a network file server in addition to its normal terminal-type function.

The approach to personal computer networking evolves in one of two ways. The first of these starting points is:

Personal computers are already in use on a stand-alone basis and the chance has now arisen to network them in order to share resources.

The second is:

A requirement for a personal computer network has been recognised. The complete network is to be installed from day one.

When considering networking from the first starting point there is little that can be done to the basic architecture of the personal computer, other than utilising add-ons. These may take the form of a second processor or an expansion chassis in order to cater for communications boards, extra memory, etc. The second starting point leaves the field for selection wide open. This is a more difficult situation, purely because of the options available, so it is here that we will explain what to look for.

At the beginning of this section the constituent parts of a basic computer were listed. These parts may be broken down further, as shown in Figure 3.3. The microprocessor consists of the CPU and possibly the clock.

The control unit is the centre of the computer's operations. It determines the sequence of operations to be performed, fetches instructions from memory, decodes them and sets up the Arithmetic and Logic Unit (ALU) for the required operations. It also handles events such as interrupts or direct memory access (DMA). The execution unit consists of a register set and the ALU. This subsystem performs the operations of shifting, comparisons, multiplication, addition, etc on the data fetched from memory.

Families of LSI chips form these basic constituent parts of the computer system. The basic parts are of course in addition to the

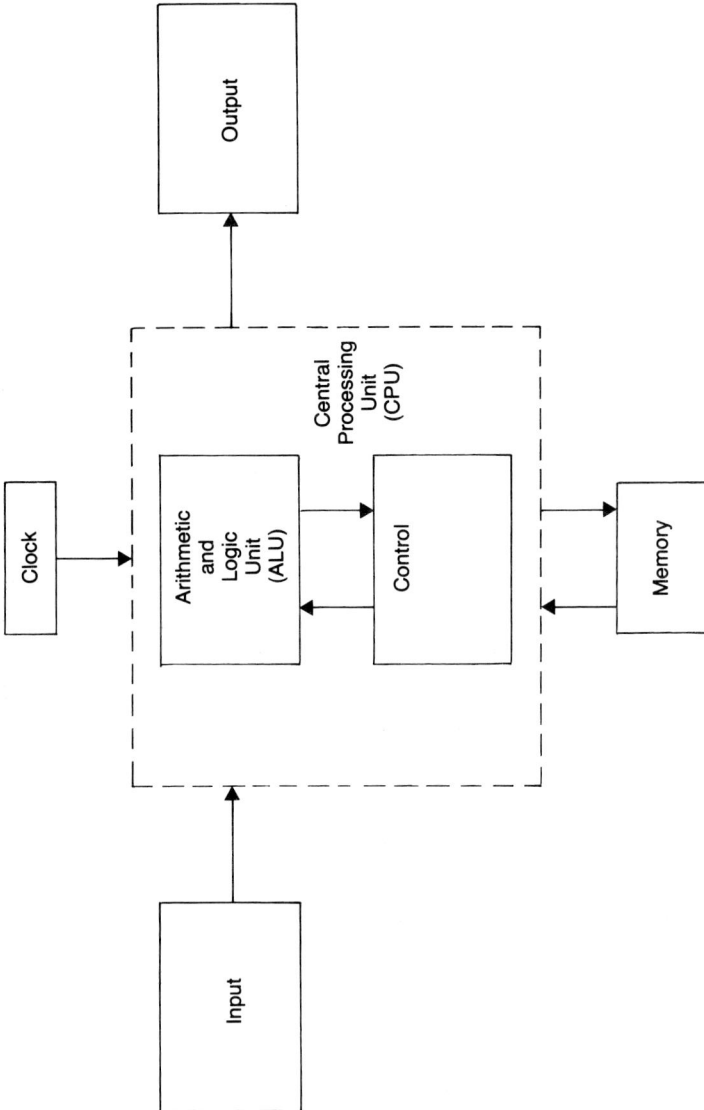

Figure 3.3   Constituent Parts of a Computer System

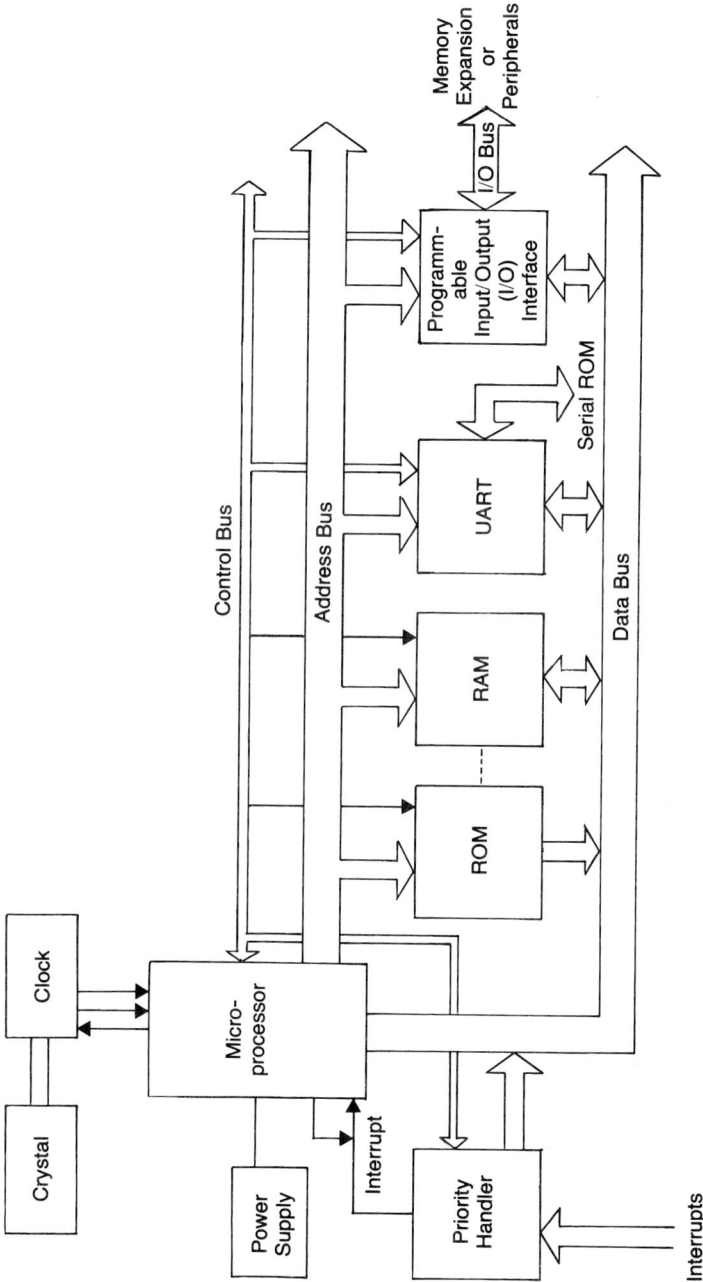

Figure 3.4 Computer System Utilising Families of LSI Chips

power supplies, etc. The architecture of a typical computer system utilising LSI techniques may be seen in Figure 3.4.

By considering Figure 3.4 in conjunction with Figure 3.2 a number of important points can be brought out to illustrate the increased power of 16-bit devices. The 8-bit devices typically require two machine cycles to transfer 16-bits of data compared with a 16-bit processor's one, hence the 16-bit will operate faster. This is a very simple explanation and the reader is left to consider and compare the features of internal architecture, data bus, data word size, etc.

Speed is not the overriding feature, as many benchmarks have shown that a personal computer containing an 8-bit microprocessor will stand up well against its 16-bit counterparts. The problem with using a personal computer as a workstation is that it may not have the technology in terms of, for example, direct memory addressing and interrupt handling.

The subsystems shown in Figure 3.4 will now be examined in order to illustrate their role in a networked (and in some cases stand-alone) personal computer environment.

The Microprocessor/Co-processor Approach to Architecture

Even taking account of the increased power of 16-bit microprocessors many tasks still tend to overload them. For this reason designs of personal computers have evolved using the co-processor approach. The co-processor approach came about because microprocessors could handle generalised data management but got bogged down when dealing with specialised functions such as extensive mathematical calculations. The tendency now is to use special chips for special functions. The co-processors can then handle various tasks – mathematical calculations, communications, graphics, etc – without placing an increased load on the host processor.

The co-processor approach for a personal computer could be important when considering applications in a networking environment in order to give it enough power to be useful. The co-processor may have been designed in from the start or may now be available as an add-on.

At this point it is worthwhile to point out the difference between tightly-coupled and loosely-coupled system architectures. This can be best illustrated by considering Figure 3.5 and Figure 3.6. These two architectures should be borne in mind and understood when looking at any hardware for the purposes of networking.

Input/Output Management Chips

Three types of management chips are briefly described:

— Programmable Interval Timer (PIT) – most microprocessor programs must generate delays which are used on output or on input to measure the time between two successive pulses. The PIT implements this software function in hardware. It is generally necessary for real-time processing when interrupts prevent the implementation of accurate timekeeping by counting;

— Programmable Interrupt Controller (PIC) – this manages multiple interrupt lines, multiple priorities and implements automatic interrupt vectoring. Automatic interrupt vectoring means that having detected and accepted an interrupt the program automatically branches to a specific address in memory where the interrupt service routine resides;

— Direct Memory Addressing Controller (DMAC) – the DMAC implements in hardware the transfer algorithms for word or block transfers between the memory and an input/output device.

The chips described above alleviate some of the tasks that the processor would normally perform.

Before looking at the actual input/output techniques we turn our attention to the memory.

Memory

Two types of memory – RAM and ROM – exist 'on-board'. The RAM is read/write volatile memory that stores both data and user-loaded programs. The user-loaded programs would be transferred from disk, cassette or other storage medium into the RAM 'work' area. It is now possible, however, to get selected user

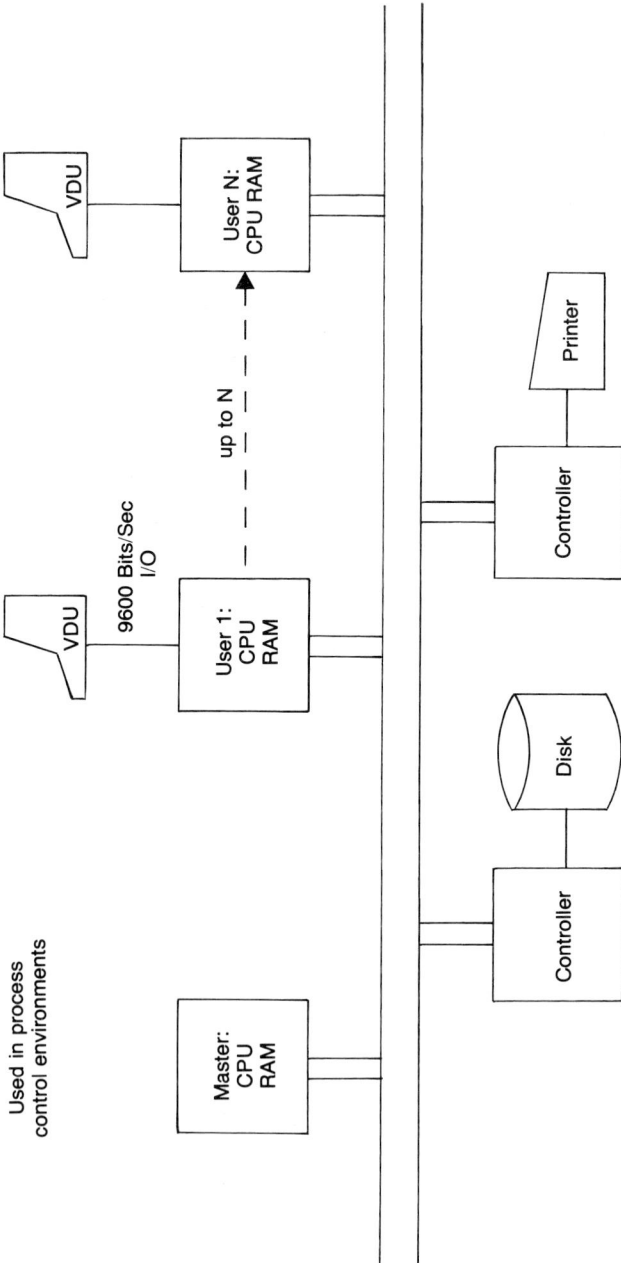

Figure 3.5 Tightly-Coupled, Multiprocessor Architecture

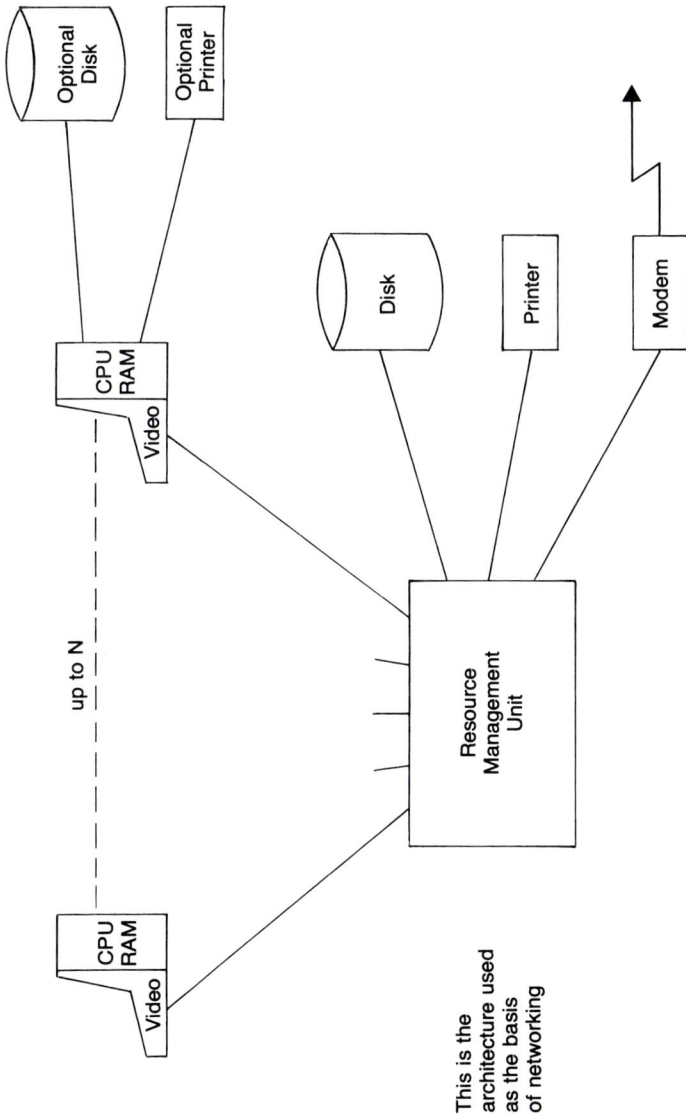

Figure 3.6 Loosely-Coupled, Multicomputer Architecture

programs such as word processing or spreadsheet packages residing directly in the personal computer. They would still be downloaded into RAM but would be much faster in doing so. The amount of directly addressable on-board RAM depends upon the number of lines given to the address. For example, the INTEL 8086 has a 20-line multiplexed address/data bus available as a 20-bit address bus, or as 16 data lines and four status lines. The 8086 can thus work on 16-bit data and has an immediate access memory range of $2^{20} = 1$ Mbyte. This is retained even when using memory mapped input/output (ie making access to the input or output look like a memory access). Note, however, that only 64K input ports and 64K output ports may be addressed during mapped operations (see Figure 3.2). Thus the address bus may be used to access 1 Mbyte of memory or the mapped ports described above.

It is important of course that sufficient memory exists in the personal computer to run the desired applications packages.

Input/Output Techniques

When connecting an input/output device to a computer system, there is a requirement for an interface, a device controller (usually a mechanical piece of equipment, eg step-motor advance), and an access technique. There are three basic access techniques: polling, interrupt and direct memory access (see Figure 3.7).

The polling technique services each device in a set pattern, even if that device does not wish to communicate. If there are a large number of input/output devices this software overhead of having to look at each device in turn can be excessive and a disadvantage. The benefits however are that the hardware for the interface is simple and because it is known exactly when each device is to be polled, it is synchronous with program execution. This is unlike the remaining two techniques which are asynchronous.

The first of these techniques is an interrupt-driven system. The interrupt from the input/output device requests processor time. Once the device generating the interrupt has been identified, the interrupt can be dealt with. Interrupts must be dealt with in a short time especially as they are normally required in real-time systems. Thus the importance of an interrupt-driven system is the speed of the microprocessor in responding to external interrupts.

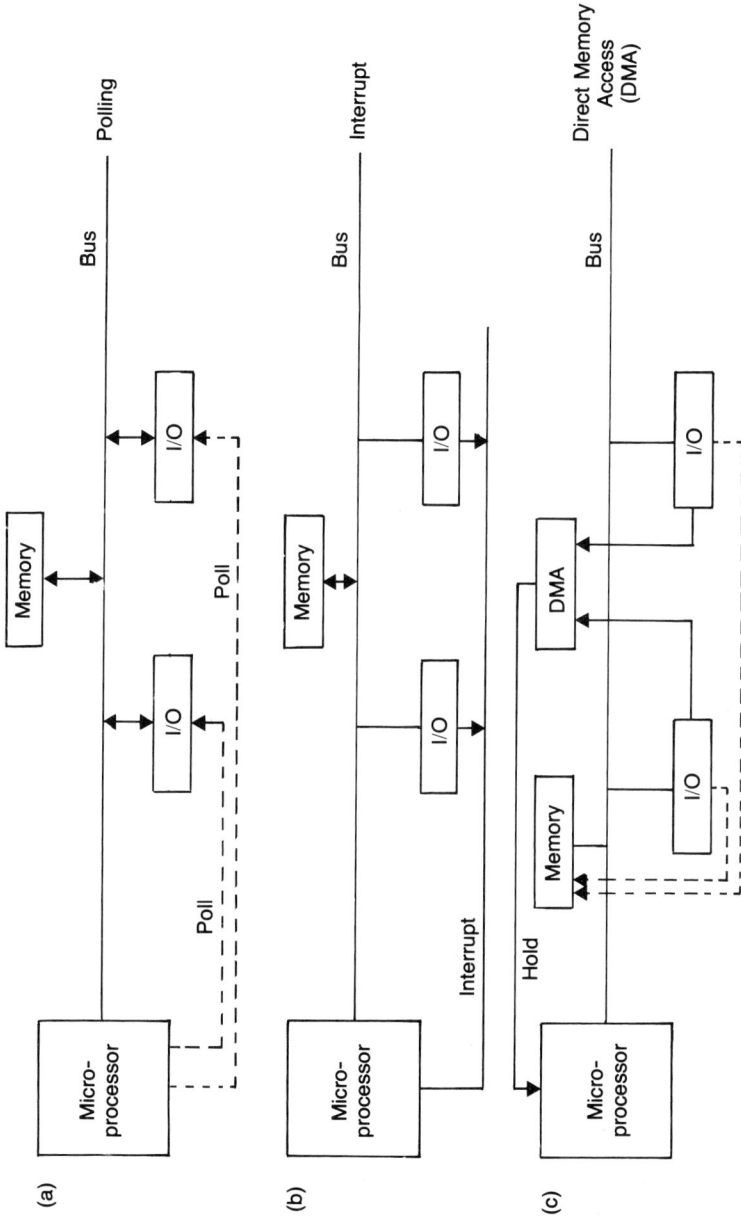

Figure 3.7 Input/Output Access Techniques

There are a number of disadvantages. Extra hardware is required if a priority interrupt system is to be used. There is also a software overhead incurred every time the interrupt routine is entered. In addition the technique operates in an asynchronous way when compared with program execution.

The second of the asynchronous techniques and the final technique to be outlined in this section is direct memory access (DMA). DMA uses a special processor which implements a block transfer. This special processor implements, automatically and, more importantly, at hardware speed a routine that would normally be executed within the microprocessor. The input/output devices, instead of sending an interrupt to the microprocessor, now send an interrupt to the direct memory access controller (DMAC). The DMA then sends a 'hold' signal to the microprocessor in order to suspend its activities and subsequently takes over control of the system in order to perform the automatic transfer of one or more words between the memory and the input/output device.

It is essential that interrupts and direct memory access are supported by personal computers if they are to be used as workstations in a network. In addition, DMA is useful for personal computer expansion, ie when adding expansion cards to the system.

To conclude this section on DMA, its advantage is that it reduces the microprocessor overhead of having to complete a memory-to-input/output-device transaction by suspending the microprocessor operation and performing the operation at hardware speed.

Input/Output Interface

The interface chips that need to be talked about and the ones that will commonly be encountered are Universal Asynchronous Receiver Transmitters (UART) and Universal Synchronous Receiver Transmitter (USRT). It is quite common to combine the asynchronous and synchronous working within one chip (USART). However, here they are considered separately.

Communications using asynchronous and synchronous formats are shown in Figure 3.8. Asynchronous transmission is not as efficient as synchronous transmission because of the requirement for start and stop bits (usually 1 start and 2 stop) for every byte of data.

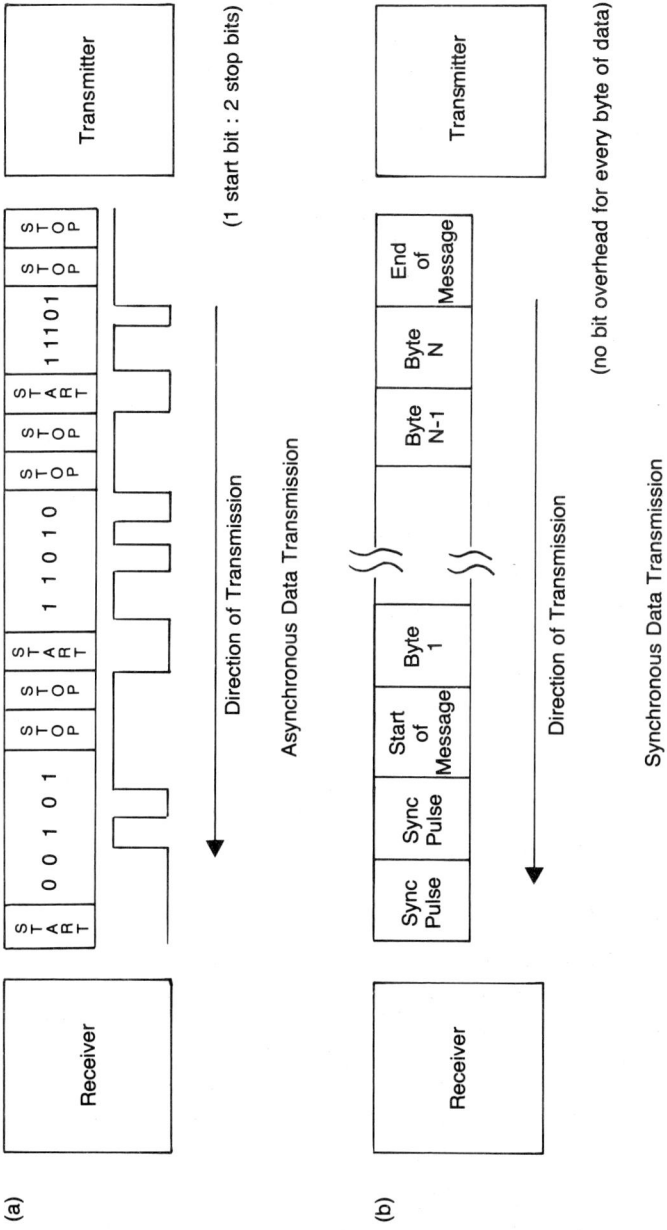

Figure 3.8 Asynchronous and Synchronous Formats

Synchronous transmission, however, has a requirement for special coding to ensure pulse transitions which add the timing element to the data.

Many devices make errors in reading and writing data. With this in mind there are three basic schemes for detecting these errors:

— *parity:* in a byte of data there is either an even or odd number of 1s occurring. The eighth bit, or sometimes an extra ninth bit, is used to make the number of 1s odd or even depending upon the type of parity to be implemented;

— *checksum:* this verifies that an entire block of data is correct by performing arithmetic (eg addition) on certain fields; frequently the bits are added using modulus arithmetic, but there are many techniques. A check character is added to the data at the end of the block. When the block is read, a new check character is generated and if this does not agree with the one in the block then an error is present within the block;

— *cyclic redundancy check:* the data bits are divided by a generator polynomial. The remainder is called the cyclic redundancy check. When the data is read, everything, including the CRC is divided by the polynomial. If the result is not zero then an error has occurred. This is a somewhat simplified explanation and the reader is directed towards the references for this chapter.

With these points in mind we can now turn our attention to UARTs and USRTs.

UARTs are used to configure the output ports of terminal devices so that they may communicate and transfer data that can be understood by both ends. It is quite common that these port configurations may be set up in hardware using dual-in-line (DIL) switches or set up in software via the keyboard. The section on applications software considers the setting up of a port from the point when the applications program is entered. This may be a definite requirement if, for example, the workstation port configurations are volatile and the workstation is powered off frequently, eg overnight.

The UART's basic function is serial/parallel conversion. Because the transmission is asynchronous it is necessary to synchronise the pulse train with an external clock signal so that successive 0s and 1s can be recognised.

The UART is split up into three sections:

— the *receiver* receives a serial input (plus clock) and translates this into a parallel output;

— the *transmitter* receives a parallel input (plus clock) and translates this into a serial output;

— the *control* receives its information from the microprocessor and carries out all of the required instructions. Status and control information can also be supplied as an output.

In addition to the serial/parallel conversion process, a UART will also perform the following functions:

— manage the start bits;

— manage the stop bits;

— verify correct data transmission using parity.

The main application of the UART is to enable the personal computer to communicate with serial devices such as a teletype, printer or modem (connected to a telephone line) using the standard RS232/V24 interface, discussed in the next section.

The USRT's basic functions and indeed its block appearance of receiver, transmitter and controller are the same as those of the UART. The USRT differs in that it is used for the synchronous transmission of data. The device would typically be connected to a modem for communication on a high-speed data line with another computer.

Interface Buses

Two interface types – serial and parallel – are considered in this section with particular emphasis on the use of a parallel interface in the form of a bus when used with personal computers.

The full interface specification provides information on the:

— electrical requirements;

— timing requirements;

— signal interrelationships;

— physical connections (and often the connectors).

The most frequently used form of *serial interface* at present is the EIA RS232C or the similar CCITT V24 interface. Newer standards such as RS422, RS423 and CCITT V35 give more reliable communications at higher speeds and over greater distances.

Serial interfaces are used to transmit data from one device to another via a single interchange circuit which is implemented with only one or two wires. A serial interface is normally a set of connections between only two devices.

The binary digits which make up a 'byte' or 'word' are transmitted serially, one after the other, down the line and are re-assembled at the other end into the 'byte' or 'word'. This requires a very simple connection needing only one signal wire plus one ground connection for one-way transmission (or two signal wires in the case of a current loop interface).

Most of the problems encountered when connecting peripherals to a personal computer via its RS232 interface come about because of the way the standard was first specified. The specification was originally meant to define the connections between DTEs and DCEs (DTE or Data Terminal Equipment is users' equipment which is joined to a data communications network. It may range from a simple terminal to a large computer system. DCE or Data Circuit Terminating Equipment describes the administration equipment at the end of a circuit and located on the customer's premises). The other side of the DCE connects to the DTE using a standard interface – for example, RS232). It is for the reason of DTE/DCE interface (necessitating the crossing over of lines) that many of us have had minor irritations at some time or other when connecting together two pieces of equipment via their RS232 ports. Simple 3-wire and 7-wire serial interfaces are shown in Figure 3.9 together with the relevant RS232 pin-outs.

A normal *parallel interface* is a set of connections between only

two devices; for example, an integrated circuit, a peripheral or a
complete computer system. Most parallel interfaces are specific to
a particular device or system but there are a small number of
standard forms such as the Centronics Printer Interface and the
BSI   Computer-Automated-Management-and-Control-Standard
(CAMAC) which cover all communication from the component
level up.

A 'bus' is a special type of parallel interface. It is designed to
allow a number of devices to be connected together at the same
time. Some popular bus standards are: IEEE 488, IEEE S100,
Intel Multibus, SS50 and VME bus.

The difference between a serial and a parallel interface is that a
parallel interface has one wire or physical connection for each 'bit'
of the computer word plus however many are required for the
control signal. The advantage of parallel buses is that the transmis-

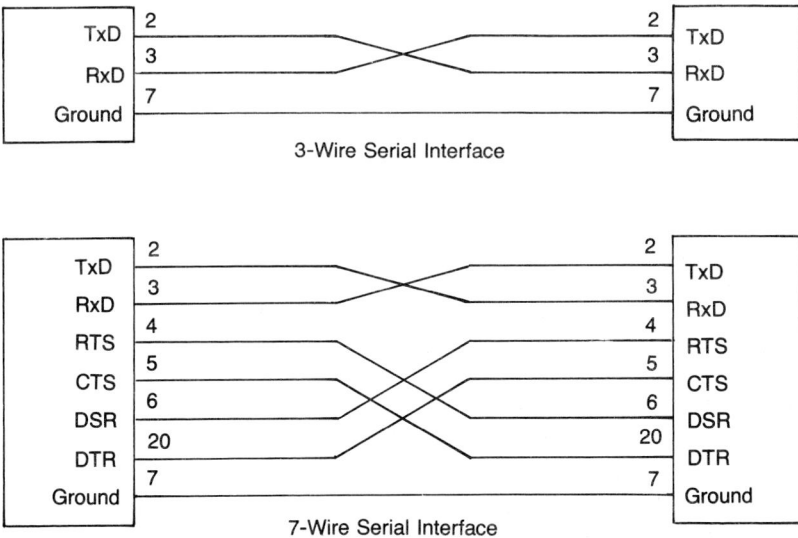

3-Wire Serial Interface

7-Wire Serial Interface

Figure 3.9   Serial Interface Connections

sion of a byte of data is faster. However, this must be offset against the cost of an increased amount of hardware to handle the data.

The IEEE-488 standard was originally intended for use in laboratory and production test environments. Indeed, production test equipment has made very good use of this standard in order to interconnect a large number of different types of manufacturers' equipment. Typically then it was used in control situations.

Each device connected to the bus could be a talker, a listener, a controller, or any combination of these three. A *talker* transmits device-dependent data to one or more listeners on the bus. Only one talker may be active at a time. A *listener* receives device-dependent data from the one active talker. There may be more than one listener active at any one time. The *controller* specifies which devices should talk or listen. The system can support more than one controller at a time, although only one may be in charge at any instant. For this reason a *system controller* is usually employed to decide which controller should be active.

Features of the IEEE-488 bus include:

— standard plug-compatible I/O bus;

— maximum of 15 devices on a bus;

— maximum of 20m of cable between all instruments on a bus;

— at least one device for every two metres of cable;

— byte serial, bit parallel, asynchronous data transfer;

— 250 kilobyte typical maximum raw data rate transfer;

— interrupt capabilities;

— block data transfer capability.

How can this be used with personal computers? The description that follows is not a network but a way of interconnecting instruments and peripherals (eg disk drives, printers, modems, plotters, etc) to a number of personal computers.

The development of integrated circuits has allowed the development of lower-cost interfaces. The benefit of the IEEE-488 bus (and often the other buses mentioned) is that it is a standard. The incorporation of IEEE-488 interfaces would therefore ensure upwards compatibility with new devices. The way this interconnection could be used in an office environment is to equip all of the personal computers with their relevant interface cards and then connect them via the IEEE-488 bus to the shared printers and disk drives. One of the personal computers would have to be designated as the system controller.

This is just an interconnection and, strictly speaking, *not* a network. However, if the limitations of cable length and number of devices are taken into account, the bus can be used for resource sharing.

The bus has been used for a number of years to connect different types of scientific and measuring instruments together. It is essentially the features of asynchronous, parallel data transfers that make it attractive. These features allow fast devices attached to the bus to go fast and slow devices to go slow.

Let me stress that this is an interface bus and not a network.

Attaching a Personal Computer to the Network

Basically the problems encountered in this area fall broadly into two categories.

The first of these is that the network and personal computers have been purchased at the same time, their advertised ability to interwork being a major factor. They could be bought from a single supplier with the personal computers classed as workstations. The main problem is in attaching too much hardware (too many personal computers) to the network. The network manufacturer may advertise a maximum number of connections. However, depending on the applications to which the network will be put, the user may experience severe degradation in network performance with only a small fraction of this hardware attached.

The second category is when the network has been bought principally to link together a number of personal computers.

A number of questions need to be asked and answered satisfactorily. These questions will undoubtedly arise in the first category also but will be tackled for the most part by the manufacturer during the design process. The questions are:

— Does the personal computer have peripheral slots? These slots are required for the interface board to the network. If only two slots are available they may be taken up for use by the network interface board and a memory expansion board for example;

— Is an expansion chassis available if all of the peripheral slots are filled? The expansion chassis may be required if, for example, an in-board modem was required in addition to the two boards mentioned above;

— What is the power requirement for the peripheral boards and is the personal computer able to supply it? Care may have to be taken when connecting in expansion chassis because of the possible introduction of external noise;

— What are the costs of the interface boards? An obvious question, maybe, but cost comparisons should be done, for example, between in-board and out-board modems;

— What ports are already available on the personal computers? This could be important when considering printer interfaces and which personal computer to use as a printer server;

— Will the individual systems be compatible? For example, if company A produces an Ethernet-compatible system it does not necessarily mean that it will connect to company B's Ethernet-compatible system. For compatibility the top four layers of the ISO 7-layer model must be the same, not just the bottom three layers covered by Ethernet (see Chapter 5);

— Are all other standards in line? This, could refer to, for example, the differing standards between CCITT and BELL with respect to modems.

Servers

If the personal computers were powerful enough it would be very nice for each to share the others' peripherals and facilities. The network could then operate very much on a peer-to-peer basis.

Powerful hardware, as discussed previously, is required to fulfil this requirement.

Additional hardware, such as mains electricity filters or isolating transformers, may be required for file servers. In a manufacturing environment a separate mains electricity feed may be required where electrical noise is a major problem (eg an arc welding plant).

Personal Computer Task Suitability

The suitability of the applications software package to perform a particular task is taken for granted as being important. This suitability will include not only efficiency and flexibility but also how user-friendly the package is. User-friendliness also relates to the hardware. User-friendliness measures the ability of an interface to bridge the gap between the human operator and the system itself. As far as the hardware is concerned, this invariably means the keyboard. For example, it may be desirable to have a separate numeric keypad if a large amount of numeric data is to be entered or indeed have provided a set of function keys for word processor applications.

The hardware cabling, repeaters, etc are discussed in the Installation section.

It is worth pointing out that the hardware usually has a requirement to fit into a specific environment. Bearing this in mind, obvious points such as size and noise must not be overlooked. In addition the hardware requirements for the network must also cover printers, eg general or letter quality. A checklist of hardware requirements may be found in Figure 3.10.

The interconnection of similar local area networks may be required and hence the availability of a suitable bridge should be investigated. A little more will be said about this in the area of fulfilling security requirements in the section on Operational and Management Requirements.

Wide Requirement

This requirement means the ability of a personal computer or microcomputer network to interconnect with and communicate

over a wide area network. (This subject is dealt with in detail in
Gandy, 1985.)

The network may support protocol converters (terminal
emulators). These must provide the following support characteristics on the link:

— electrical;

— signal configurations;

— pin assignments.

Communication over a wide area network usually requires a
modem. The choice may be in-board (residing in the personal
computer or workstation and taking up an expansion slot) or

NETWORK COMPONENT	CHECKLIST/AVAILABILITY
Personal Computer/ Workstation	— microprocessor used — co-processor — direct addressing capability — direct memory addressing — peripheral expansion slots — expansion chassis — power capability (watts) — input/output management — ports available — separate network port available — separate keyboard numeric pad — function keys (programmable)
Servers	— file server — print server — name server (user name, network address, mapping) — time server (time and date from real-time clock) — gateway server — mail — telex — viewdata
Peripheral Equipment	— modems (in-board, out-board, standards) — printers (general for spool and/or letter quality)

Figure 3.10   Checklist of Hardware Requirements

out-board (the modem usually sits by the telephone with an inter-connection to the personal computer). The modem may be used as a 'pool' resource by other personal computers on the network. Communication over a wide area network may also come about by using an acoustic coupler together with a portable personal computer.

Once again standards are a major factor in wide area communications and include differences in modems with CCITT and BELL specifications.

As discussed previously, just as a bridge fulfils a local need, a gateway fulfils the wide area need.

SOFTWARE REQUIREMENTS

The software requirements of the network discussed in this section are considered by splitting them up into two basic parts: the software and methods required for the local operation of the network, and the software and methods required for the wide operation of the network (ie when there is a need to go outside the network in order to gain access to the desired information).

Local Requirements

Applications Software

The applications software is one of the most important considerations when selecting a system to perform a particular task. This section looks at two areas:

— adapting single user packages for network use;

— application program generators (APGs).

The next section on the operating system software mentions the applications packages. Because the number of available applications packages is changing so rapidly, the reader should consult the software directories (NCC Microsystems Centre).

The reason why the two areas (adapting single user packages and APGs) are considered is that the organisation installing the network does not have the resources for software development. It does not matter if the organisation is large or small. The larger organisation may have made a conscious decision to address the software problems as the network could well be running as a pilot scheme for possible inclusion into the overall corporate strategy.

Adapting Single User Packages for Network Use

Networks really come to the fore when multi-user software is available on them. This allows the users to share the programs and data and not just the hardware resource. Adapting single user packages to run as multi-user on a personal computer network is a difficult process, although a number of software packages run in this way. In general this modification is in the hands of the application software suppliers.

For the most part the network suppliers have concentrated on communications and resource sharing, ignoring the problems of the multi-user environment. There is a basic difference between multi-user on a network and multi-user operating systems on personal computers. Multi-user network systems must manage the communications and support the applications far more.

True multi-user software on a network will allow one user to update an individual record in a file while other users still have access to the rest of the file's data (Figure 3.11).

Clearly if access to a specific record is required then the action must be to check if that record is free and, if it is, to set its condition to be locked. A further action evident from this process is to ensure that no two users are able to lock the same record. To implement this process there must be some sort of co-operation from the network file server.

There are a number of systems on the market which implement partition locking rather than record locking. A partition is that part of a file server's disk that has been designated for use by specific applications programs and users. The partition designations are set up at the planning stage. The hard disk is divided up 'cake-like' between intended users of the system. Partition locking limits the access to applications programs unless the system partitions are set up very carefully. It can be set up in various ways. One way is to give each partition holding the software a certain status. This status may be 'read-only', 'read-write', etc. The users then have their access rights set up. This can work perfectly well but has the limitation that the same software may have to be duplicated on more than one partition in order to preserve its integrity when more than one user requires access. This type of system requires careful thought and consideration as to which users require access to which software, so that the network does not merely end up as a centralised storage system.

Taking the idea of user and partition access rights one step

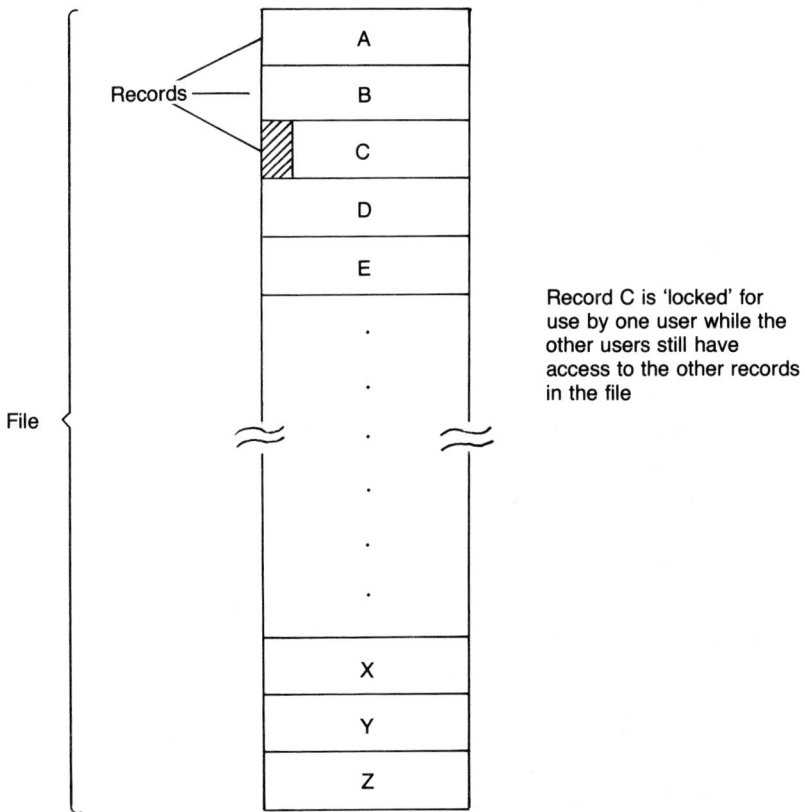

Record C is 'locked' for use by one user while the other users still have access to the other records in the file

Figure 3.11   Record Locking

further, rather than setting these up at a central network manager, it would be of more use to change the access rights from a remote user terminal. This comes down to locking the partition. The way it may work is that a remote terminal may request access to a partition in use. The terminal currently using that partition is informed of the fact by a semaphore (or flag) appearing on the screen. The problem with this system is that the terminal currently using the partition cannot be forced to relinquish control. Hence the requesting terminal may be locked-out from gaining access to a large amount of relevant applications software. Our attentions must once again turn to record locking in order to:

— minimise duplicated applications software;

— minimise user frustration when confronted with a lock-out situation.

It should be said that partition access is perfectly adequate in a large number of cases, providing both the work and applications software lend themselves to be sensibly structured on a hard disk's partitions.

Record locking may be implemented on personal computer networks in the following ways:

— 'active' record locking;

— file server – 'exclusive use';

— 'passive' record locking – 'semaphores'.

During 'active' record locking the lock takes place when the user *reads* the record not when the change has been completed and it is ready to be written back. The lock is implemented after consulting the status of the record from an index table and before the contents of the record are read from disk. The locking action which includes, as an inherent part, access to the index table must utilise a semaphore to indicate that no other user may even gain access to the index table while it is currently being uniquely used. This use of the semaphore will remove the possibility of multiple locking of a single record. The single user applications software may then be used in the normal way. Having used the software the unlock routine must reverse the process giving access for other users. This reversal of the process must obviously ensure that the record is unlocked only after the amendment has been completed.

The implementation of exclusive use of the file server on a temporary basis is a very necessary feature on networks supporting multi-user software. This exclusive use enables the environment to support a number of locking arrangements, in turn making the software more portable by calling a command such as 'exclusive use' within the applications software provided the facility is supported by the network supplier.

'Passive' record locking using the network's semaphores may be used to indicate exclusive access to a record. The semaphore routine in this case will be run by the file server and a 'call' will be made to this routine in order to implement a record locking structure.

If the network does now have multi-user capabilities, careful consideration must be made concerning the system's response time and its relationship to the number of active users. This will be expanded in the section on operating systems.

Application Program Generators (APGs)

Application software is purchased to suit a specific application requirement. The availability of individual application packages, such as the various spreadsheet and database packages, depends upon both the operating system under which they will run (operating systems will be discussed in a separate section) and the hardware configuration for which the operating system is available. Here attention is given to application program generators and how they may be used to automate some of the development work.

Personal computer networks are relatively cheap and may be installed into environments where there is little or no computer expertise. It is essential in these situations that either:

— applications software is bought in complete, requiring no development, or

— if development is required, it is simple.

The use of application program generators will alleviate some of the workload of software development in small companies as well as reducing the dependency on the data processing department in large businesses.

APGs make savings in two ways. Firstly, almost all APG products are on-line development tools and so there is no lost time waiting for programs to be run. Secondly, APGs automate the code production phase of software development. The APG provides general solutions and performs very well in the area of general coding (eg data declarations, input handling, file handling and report formatting). The APG does not perform well, however, in the area of specific applications.

Reduced software development times are often more important in personal computer networks because there is a desire to get them installed and working as quickly as possible. In addition the cost of the software development becomes of increasing importance. It is little use trying to get a smaller (and less powerful) system to do the job of a larger system less efficiently just because of the initial purchase price.

APGs provide the user with a menu-driven generator which provides options from which the user selects the appropriate one. The final output is a BASIC program which has been compiled. Alternatively the APG may hold programs as a series of operations which are interpreted at run time.

The 'automatic' production of programs using an APG does remove some but not yet all of the expertise from programming. In addition an APG does supply general rather than specific solutions to problems. Nevertheless for certain applications they can prove most useful and should certainly be considered if the software development of applications packages is to be attempted on a personal computer network.

This section has thus looked at applications software, in particular, adapting single user packages for network use (identifying the modifications required) and applications program generators for their use in developing applications software packages.

User-Friendly?

In addition to operating systems and hardware requirements (eg does my personal computer have enough memory for it to run the applications program?), there can be a number of pitfalls and opportunities. The opportunities stem from the number of available software packages running under the relevant operating system software. An essential item, and in fact an underlying theme, is that the applications software is above all user-friendly, a requirement which can be attributed to the overall system and not merely the software. The software must also suit the requirement to which it is being put, a point that cannot be stressed too strongly. A user-friendly system can have an immense impact on the amount of training required.

Operating System Software

We have seen how an applications package can be modified to provide record locking. Some co-operation from the file server is required to achieve this. The outcome would be a network that would allow several users to share a file, or indeed a database, without the system getting fouled up because of attempted multiple accesses to the same information. The point to note is that work is required by the end user or software supplier in order to compensate for a deficiency in the operating system software.

This section examines the requirement of operating systems to be used for personal computers and also the requirement of operating systems for networks. To understand the operating system requirements for networks, it is helpful to understand the operating system requirements for personal computers. This includes an explanation of multi-user and concurrency, qualifying them by the context in which they are discussed (ie supporting single users or providing multi-user support).

Personal Computer Operating Systems

One function of an operating system is to act as a link between the application software and the computer hardware. It allows the user to get on with using the applications package (a spreadsheet, database, etc) without worrying how the disk directories are organised or which peripherals are attached to which ports. Operating systems take care of these and many other functions.

The operating system under consideration can be evaluated by considering four general requirement areas:

— programming efficiency
    — choice of good languages?
    — debugging and editing tools?
    — easy to write?

— operating efficiency
    — amount of memory left for applications?
    — data transfer time to disks?
    — will applications software run quickly?

— portability
    — is it available on a number of systems?
    — can software be transported to another system?

— ease of use
    — are there sensible error messages?
    — is it easy for the operator to use the applications programs?
    — can it support more than one screen (and processor) at a time?

No operating system provides complete answers to all of the above questions. If it did, the choice would be much simpler.

In addition, other actions that must be implemented by an operating system include:

— input/output control;

— random access memory organisation;

— assign devices to physical ports;

— provide operator interaction;

— provide disk handling facilities;

— provide file handling facilities;

— provide job stream, batch, or submit processing commands;

— provide programming tools;

— monitor and process hardware interrupts;

— provide a password protection scheme.

The popular operating system designed to provide a solution for systems based on the Intel 8080 and later the Zilog Z80 micro-processors was CP/M from Digital Research. This operating system got in on the ground floor which explains why so many applications packages were written using it – it was available and it worked. The problem remained that CP/M was limited to single-user systems.

The use of personal computers has evolved from so-called 'microcomputers' that provided a huge extension to the office calculator function. To be used effectively in a business environment the personal computer must satisfy three needs (or at least have the potential to do so):

— *personal:* the user's own files and requirements;

— *local:* the user's own departmental needs;

— *wide:* the user's corporate needs.

The needs can be set up in a hierarchy as shown in Figure 3.12.

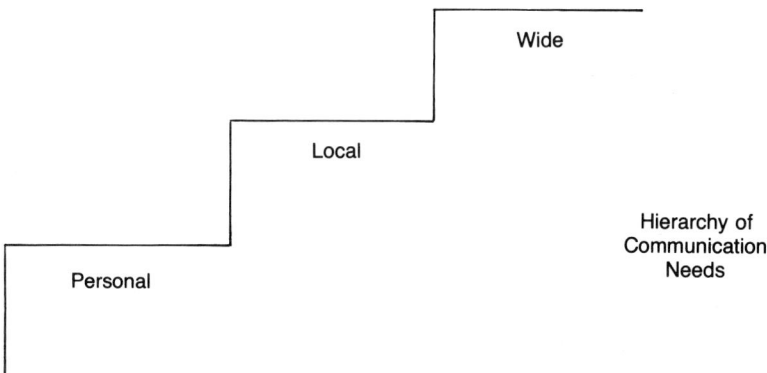

Wide

Local

Hierarchy of
Communication
Needs

Personal

Figure 3.12   Hierarchy Showing the Needs Satisfied by a Personal Computer

The amount of hardware and software at each level varies as needs are satisfied, as does the communication needs at each level. For example, a stand-alone personal computer complete with a terminal emulator package and relevant hardware may satisfy the needs at all levels by providing local computing facilities and access to corporate, or external, facilities. However, needs at individual levels do not remain fixed for all time. When a computer is installed, people have an 'exponential expectation' of the system's ability. This results in a required growth pattern, not merely of computing power but also of the communications facilities.

Single-user operating systems are becoming a hindrance to the growth pattern in certain situations. In addition to this the hardware development of 16-bit microprocessors, and their subsequent use in systems, have stimulated the development of more powerful machines.

The advent of 16-bit microprocessors brought about a requirement for 16-bit operating systems. The requirement was met and two of the more familiar 16-bit operating systems were developed: CP/M86 from Digital Research, and MSDOS from Microsoft (the suppliers of the industry standard MBASIC). MSDOS is used by IBM in practically the same form under the name of PCDOS. The important fact to note is that both CP/M86 and MSDOS are still single-user systems.

In order to fully utilise the power of the 16-bit micro a multi-tasking operating system was required (one such example is Concurrent CP/M86). Multi-tasking operating systems allow the computer to perform more than one job at a time. For example, printing out a listing while performing a calculation or a network communications function. (Much of the efficiency in performing multi-tasking and multi-user operations depends upon the architecture of the computer hardware.) Concurrent CP/M86 still operates in a single-user environment.

UNIX developed by Bell Laboratories was largely discarded for multi-user applications with the advent of the 8-bit microprocessor because of its size. However, with the advent of the more powerful 16-bit microprocessors it has become a more viable proposition, despite its size. UNIX has been implemented on a number of personal computers, although it does require a hard disk drive in order to provide it with a home. The access to files in UNIX is on a hierarchical basis making much easier the control of the file security, and so preventing unauthorised persons from entering the system. A major problem with UNIX is that there is no record locking facility, meaning that two users can gain access to the same piece of data at the same time and corrupt or destroy it. The previous section described how to implement this facility in the applications package. The correct solution is to provide a facility for record locking within the operating system. Suppliers of UNIX systems have to write their own record locking routines. Take care if a UNIX implementation is to be considered because of its inherent problems.

It is useful to summarise the major operating systems currently available for personal computers (see Figure 3.13). In some respects the choice of an operating system is academic as the computer is a tool and the choice of a computer system may be based upon:

— identifying the applications packages best suited to your needs;

— noting down which operating system they run on;

— selecting a hardware configuration which will support the operating system.

However, it is best to be armed with some knowledge of operating systems, if only for consideration of the flexibility and future expansion of the chosen computer system. Future versions of Concurrent CP/M (Concurrent DOS) and UNIX should have the edge.

Network Operating Systems

In order to support multi-user applications and the distributed functions inherent in networks the network operating system requires special features. Chapter 5 describes the standards situation while Chapter 4 describes network topologies (eg star, loop, ring, bus), network access methods (eg CSMA/CD, token passing, etc) and transmission media (eg coaxial cable, twisted pair, etc). It is the job of the network operating system to integrate all of these

OPERATING SYSTEM	ADVANTAGES	DISADVANTAGES	COMMENTS
CP/M 8-bit	large software base; easy to implement on newly designed machines; CP/M plus has tree structured directories and better help facilities	poor error messages; hard for new-comers to use	an integrated chip from ZILOG incorporating Personal CP/M in ROM and a Z80 processor should make it attractive to the home-user market
CP/M 16-bit	Concurrent CP/M provides multi-tasking and windows for single users; powerful good range of software; easy for CP/M (8-bit) users to get used to; CP/M-68K for 68000 based machines (competing with UNIX)	concurrent version requires powerful hardware (also Concurrent DOS); poor user interface	concurrency and multi-tasking facilities are ideal for office automation use
MSDOS	XENIX (based on UNIX) is the multi-user product; large software base; tree-structured directories; fairly good error messages	only runs on 8086 and 8088 machines	known as PC-DOS on the IBM PC; IBM seem to prefer UNIX to XENIX; now running on most new 16-bit office systems; MSX-DOS is the disk operating system for the Japanese 8-bit MSX machine
UNIX	multi-tasking provides good tools for programmers; software is very portable; really need it written in 'C' for portability	needs a large amount of disk space; runs on 68000-based systems; the 68000 has proper memory management not much commercial software user-unfriendly interface	well established in the technical environments; started as multi-user minicomputer operating system now becoming available on micros; no record locking though
APPLE DOS	large software base; small memory requirement	limited to APPLE and look-alikes	tied to APPLE developments; useful as the operating system for cheap 8-bit machines

Figure 3.13   A Summary of Major Operating Systems Currently Available for Personal Computers

OPERATING SYSTEM	ADVANTAGES	DISADVANTAGES	COMMENTS
UCSD P-SYSTEM	good software portability; established in higher education; widely available; good range of programmer's tools	limited amount of business software; Pascal and Fortran supported but few other languages	portability is its prime aim, ie from 8-bit to 16-bit and even to PDP-11s; may suit running under UNIX from a compiled intermediate code
PICK	easy for user; built-in database; fast; good for system developers; virtual memory management	available only on a few micros (it was originally a mini operating system) as it is new in this area; mainly available on 68000-based machines	possibly will be used within large corporations to most advantage
OASIS	multi-user; available in 8-bit and 16-bit versions; easy to use; good development facilities; good security features; range of file types	not much software	it is said to rival UNIX in facilities but is easier to use for the end user; C, COBOL and compiled BASIC are supported
BOS	working multi-user system for micros; very portable	limited software base; limited to one dialect of COBOL	business-oriented multi-user operating system linked to Microcobol
Integrated Operating Systems	easy to learn to use; software is usually integrated	software base is small; requires powerful hardware; can be slow; frustrating to use once the basic concepts have been mastered	operating systems and application programs merge into one; conventional operating systems will drift this way; multi-tasking environment often uses a mouse to control a pointer on the screen; APPLE's LISA and MACINTOSH and ICL's PERQ use integrated operating systems

Figure 3.13   A Summary of Major Operating Systems Currently Available for Personal Computers (Continued)

into a fully functioning and usable system. At the moment not much attention has been given to integrating network capabilities into existing operating systems.

A system must integrate all of the capabilities it is presented with in order to provide the user with a consistent set of commands. The hardware details must remain invisible to the end user, existing merely as a facility on the network. By making the network transparent, applications software can run without any modification, just as if it were running on a single stand-alone system.

The personal computer can be thought of as an expanding world with its own horizon. The more the world expands, the more the entity contained within the world comes into contact with interactive elements. A stand-alone personal computer can use its own operating system in its own world. A network, however, must encompass all of the entities within its world so that to the applications program it functions as if it was a stand-alone personal computer. In this way the network becomes completely transparent to the applications software.

The software structure is arranged in layers comprising sections of code which pass information between themselves. The BIOS layer controls the hardware and interfaces to another layer (a standard layer) called the BDOS. This layer in turn communicates with the applications programs. The BIOS will typically be loaded with all of the device drivers necessary for a particular product.

When a number of personal computers are connected to form a network the applications program passes an instruction to the operating system, just as if it were still in a stand-alone device. Now, however, the operating system must intervene in order to ensure that the instructions are sent to the correct peripheral. This intervention is required in order to make the most use of the distributed hardware that is resident on the network.

Devices on the network can be servers (offering themselves to be used by other devices) or requestors (asking if they may use other devices). It is a good idea to have dedicated file and printer servers when there is a chance that the servers may receive a large number of requests. This necessity for dedication becomes apparent if the file server, for example, is combined with an end-user device. The centralised servers avoid the duplication of both software and system utilities.

The operating system must also deal with the execution of a program using a remote processor. This means the user running a processor other than the one to which he is directly connected. The remote processor must access facilities as if it was the user's own local processor.

Record locking, another aspect of the operating system's requirements, is provided by many network operating systems as a facility in the file server. The file server knows the physical location of the data on the disk. Record locking may be presented in a number of ways:

— physical record locking: prevents the access to records in a physical area of the disk while one is being updated.

— logical record locking: prevents the access to a file while a record within it is being updated.

— virtual record locking: does not prevent access but flags the address of a record that is already being updated.

With virtual record locking applications programs must acknowledge the flag and act on it. The result of not doing this is almost certainly a 'BDOS' error.

When providing a locking facility the network should ensure that a lock-out condition, resulting in no-one being able to gain access to a particular record, will not occur. DR NET is network software that will prove to be a major factor for all independent network suppliers as Concurrent DOS takes over from MS-DOS. DR NET will provide the interface into Concurrent DOS, providing the control required from the network operating system.

The final requirement considered here is that of security. Networks should allow flexibility in that some files will be more public than others. Passwords may be required on the network for these and other reasons. The use of bridges to supply a measure of security is discussed in the section on 'Operational and Management Requirements'.

Wide Requirements

The inclusion of this topic acknowledges the fact that at some time in the future they will want to use the network to gain access to external data. The external data may be in such a location as to require the intermediate use of a wide area network, the access to which is usually gained by means of a gateway.

The function of gateways has already been described in Chapter 1. The applications in Chapter 2 described the possible uses in gaining access to information in external databases. Combining these two, and building on our knowledge of gateways, what does this mean as far as the software requirement goes?

Firstly we have learned that in order to gain access to an external system we must have the correct hardware configuration. This means that the port we want to communicate over must be correctly set up for bit rate, parity etc, suggesting that the software used to gain access to the external facilities is user friendly. On entering the software routine, it should in itself set up the relevant port configuration.

Secondly, having set up the hardware requirement for communications, the applications software should present no indication to the user which protocol is being used for end-to-end transmission. It may be ICL's CO3 or IBM's SNA or one of many others but it should not matter. The network should present itself as being totally transparent to the end-user.

Good communications software is the key to a flexible system. The detail of a micro-to-mainframe connection is a subject in its own right. A full discussion of this subject is contained in Gandy, 1985, and the requirements of communication software are set out as a summary in Figure 3.14. The summary shows the actions to be performed, in order to achieve the required information flow. Within each section some key points are outlined. The six sections may be broken down as follows:

— communication package selection;

— pre-communication set-up;

ACTION	KEY POINTS
Communication Package Selection	available packages may operate under a CP/M86, MSDOS (PCDOS) or some other operating systems; many only operate under one; files downloaded under CP/M86 will not be accessible from MSDOS because the disk formats are not the same
Pre-Communication Set-Up	the communication ports' parameters must be set up; these include: — bit rate; — number of data bits; — type of parity check; — number of start bits; — number of stop bits; Half-duplex and full-duplex switchable configuration
Initiating the Communications Session	manual set-up of the connection using a manual modem; automatic set-up using an auto-dial modem; includes listing the telephone numbers available for the auto-dial modem; switchable modes for originate and answer facilities; ability to upgrade to higher bit rate modems without major upheaval
The Communications Session	download – capture directly to disk or capture to memory, transferring to disk later; upload – transfer from disk to the remote host system; XON/XOFF is a speed matching protocol used to control the transmission of data when a buffer is getting full. data capture to the printer is a means of printing out the data as it is being received; selective printing is useful; listing directories of all disk drives is a useful feature when uploading files and downloading files; OFF-LINE/ON-LINE are necessary for dealing with changes or enquiries without breaking the link with the host; error handling facilities should be built-in for example issuing a warning concerning the possible loss of data
Concluding the Communications Session	the software should return elegantly to the operating system, without requiring a system reboot, at the end of the session; a 'BREAK KEY' function may be required in order to immediately interrupt an executing program
Documentation References	a help file that can be entered at any time during the session is an important feature; good user manuals are also important

Figure 3.14   Summary of Communications Software Requirements

— initiating communications;

— communication process;

— concluding communications;

— support facilities.

The six sections are meant to give the reader a brief outline of some of the points to watch when setting up, or considering setting up, a communications link.

INSTALLATION REQUIREMENTS

Having decided upon and purchased the personal computer network components – which may comprise a network file server, a print server, several personal computer interface cards and the necessary cable and terminators – the next stage is to install it.

The installation of the network, whether performed by the network supplier or a third party nominated by the network supplier, is a source of a great many hidden costs. If the complete installation of the network is performed by the purchaser then it is essential that a good technical back-up is provided by the supplier if and when problems occur. In many instances it is part of the contract that installing the cable may be left to the purchaser, providing the supplier's guidelines are followed.

The direct costs of the network itself have added to them the indirect costs of the installation. The stages of installation which go towards making up these indirect costs are, for example:

— planning the network configuration;

— labour costs for cable and tap installation;

— installing the software;

— debugging;

— software modification;

— staff training.

The final two points covering program conversion and staff

training have been mentioned in the sections in this chapter entitled 'software requirements' and 'user-friendly?' respectively. It is important, however, to briefly restate their importance in the context of network installation. Many applications software packages may require modifications in order that they may be put to full use in a network environment. The modification may provide record or file locking facilities in order that a single package, resident on a network, may be sensibly accessed by more than one user. This whole process stems from the basic misconception of the differences between 'multi-user' on a network and 'multi-user' operating systems on personal computers. In addition to the modification mentioned above there may be a requirement to modify software which is incompatible with the new system. It is hoped that this will be a very small requirement indeed!

The other area is staff training, tied very closely to the user-friendliness of the chosen devices. A great deal of time and money can be spent if the devices chosen are not user-friendly.

The two points above will also come to light when considering the choice of a network. Before considering the mechanics of installation, one must be aware that the indirect costs may well exceed the direct costs.

If the user is intending cabling the network there are a number of points to consider. These relate to the actual cable used. For example, will the user test all of the installed cables for transmission loss, ensuring that they comply with the manufacturer's recommendations? For broadband systems using coaxial cable this may include measuring the transmission and return loss using a radio frequency sweep generator. If the installation uses optical fibre then couplings of fibre-to-fibre, fibre-to-source and fibre-to-detector must be made and tested carefully. For baseband systems it is essential to test the electrical continuity of the cable both before and after installation.

Before the cable is installed the network's configuration must be carefully planned. All distances must be carefully measured. It is a common mistake to underestimate the amount of cable required by as much as 100%, ie twice as much cable was required than first thought, in order to allow for bends, drops, etc.

The planning of the network's configuration depends very much on the topology of the chosen system, ie whether it is a bus or a ring etc, the facilities of the building in which it is to be installed, and finally the cabling constraints imposed by the design of the network itself.

The limitations imposed on the network's configuration by the design of the network may cover such areas as:

— how far terminals can be from the main cable;

— distance between tapping points on the main cable;

— maximum cable length (end-to-end);

— maximum cable length between repeaters;

— ease of providing new tapping points not designed in from the start;

— ease of expansion (extra cable lengths), and the problems these may pose for reconfiguring the network (eg a clock unit may be required to sit in or near the centre of the cable run).

Having now established that the design of the network can in itself impose limitations we shall turn our attention towards the cabling part of the installation.

The design of the cable system should allow each device to be attached to the network in the easiest way possible. It should be designed so that it is flexible in order that equipment can be easily moved to other locations, and also that it can be easily expanded in order to cater for future requirements. These points will vary in order of importance.

There are basically four cable installation techniques which are in common use today:

— under floor cabling;

— over ceiling cabling;

— surface mounted raceway cabling;

— existing wall ducts.

A single installation may comprise any one or all four of these techniques.

The under-floor technique may use ducts, installed when the building was erected, or a raised floor, installed afterwards. The raised or false floor is typically used in mainframe computer environments when no provision of cabling ducts had been made from the outset. The use of ducts, where available, does provide a certain amount of physical security.

The over-ceiling cabling is of most use in the type of environment that uses removable ceiling tiles. The installation of the cable will be cheaper than that of under floor cabling and makes a system much easier to expand. There may be obstacles such as air conditioning and electrical cables to avoid because of the potential hazards of noise being introduced into unshielded network cable through external electromagnetic sources.

The surface-mounted raceway cabling technique has the cable running around the perimeter of a room. This may make it necessary for the terminal equipment itself to be located around the perimeter of the room. Choosing a metal type of raceway will provide a certain amount of shielding from undesirable external electromagnetic noise.

Existing wall ducts tend to be used less often unless they are physically large enough to allow the cable to be installed comfortably. Quite often this type of ducting negotiates right angle bends making small ducting unsuitable for some cable types. There is no need in some instances to use raceways and the cable may be simply tied directly to the surface of the wall. This technique does, however, make the cable susceptible to accidental damage.

The network history including cable routeing, taps, repeaters and peripherals should have both their locations and installation details clearly documented, possibly on the system itself, providing hard copy is available for security purposes.

The following ten points summarise the cable installation procedure:

1   Route cables so that they are easily accessible. This will make future expansion, maintenance or reconfiguring the network

easier. Be aware of electrically noisy environments.

2   Mark the head-end side of amplifiers, taps and splitters on broadband systems (see Chapter 4).

3   Mark the tap points on the cable of baseband systems such as Ethernet or any system specifying a minimum distance between taps.

4   Attach all cable equipment solidly to the building so that the cable itself does not have to support their weight.

5   Support the weight of the cable approximately every 5 metres (depending on the cable weight per unit length) when it is not supported by conduit, ducting or raceway.

6   Terminate unused cable ends, where appropriate, with the relevant impedance.

7   Keep cables in a dry environment with their ends sealed.

8   Do not exceed the minimum bending radius of the cable.

9   Do not exceed the maximum pulling force of the cable, nor twist it excessively during installation.

10   Test cable continuity and performance before and after installation. For large networks install and test in sections.

By adhering to the above ten points the subsequent software installation and system debugging should flow much more smoothly. These ten points serve as guidelines even if the actual cable installation work is not being performed by the actual end-user.

It now only remains to discuss the problems which may arise from using certain types of equipment in certain types of environment. Noisy equipment inside the office can have a bad effect on personnel. It is important to appreciate that seemingly small problems can achieve large dimensions.

When planning the network ensure that noisy devices such as printers are strategically placed and suitably muffled. Complete enclosures can be purchased for this purpose. Consider the environmental requirements for each piece of equipment at the planning stage. For example, do not put the network file server in a smokey or dusty atmosphere where the filters of the system are likely to clog and require more frequent cleaning. Or worse still, the heads crash and the system becomes inoperable. Attention to details such as these at the planning stage will make the operation and management of the system, discussed in the next section, very much easier. Figure 3.15 provides a summary chart of the installation procedure. The basic installation guide may be thought of as consisting of the following three stages:

— decide where the equipment is to be situated;

— cable up to the equipment;

— install the software and debug.

The installation procedure chart (Figure 3.15) merely adds some meat on to the bare bones of the three stages above. The install software stage does include setting up the systems' users, which should have been thought out at the planning stage. This could consist of, for instance, deciding on the size, type and operating system for each required partition, deciding on the optimum size of the spool file, partition, etc.

OPERATIONAL AND MANAGEMENT REQUIREMENTS

It is this area where many users find both hidden costs and, in some instances, the fact that their network will not function in the way they want it to.

The management requirements of a network relate not only to the day-to-day management of security back-ups, dealing with enquiries, etc, but also setting up the system from the installation stage.

The subjects involved in the operational and management requirements will now be looked at. Some attention will be given to the management structure required for reporting faults and dealing with enquiries. This is a particularly important area for larger companies endeavouring to develop and follow a corporate company policy.

All of the following subjects coming under the ultimate control

EQUIPMENT	PLANNING CONSIDERATIONS	INSTALLATION	TEST AND DEBUG
hardware — peripheral equipment; PCs; controller; printers; servers	office layout requirements; network topology; future requirements	avoid dusty environments; special requirements? eg temperature; humidity easy access for maintenance and security back-up; special requirements for noisy printers; power requirements (mains filters or isolating transformers?); any other pre-installation work eg air conditioning to be phased in	where possible test all equipment in stand-alone mode initially; run debug and diagnostic routines; run test routines, eg printer – character set print PC – memory check RAM – verify disk and diskettes
hardware cabling equipment cable; amplifiers; taps and splitters; head-ends (broadband)	office layout requirements; maximum distance requirements; future tap requirements; flexibility	make cables easy to access (beware of noisy environments); mark head-end side of equipment connected to broadband systems; mark tap points; attach equipment solidly to building; support cable weight adequately; terminate cable ends with relevant impedance; keep cables dry; do not exceed minimum bending radius of cable; do not exceed maximum pulling force of cable, nor twist it excessively during installation; power requirements for non-line powered taps	test cable continuity before installation; test cable continuity after installation; on large systems test during stages of installation; for broadband systems special equipment is required, eg RF sweep generator or optical fibre test equipment

software	decide who requires which type of application package and choose a suitable one;
	
	are there any operating system considerations?
	
	use the selection criteria outlined in Chapter 6 (Choosing a Microcomputer Network)
	eg – user-friendly;
	    – response time;
	    etc
		install the relevant software on the relevant partition having first structured the system;
		
		set up the users;
		
		put their identities on the network;
		
		set up the network facilities eg electronic mail etc
			run applications packages;
			
			run network facilities;
			
			this results in much more of a system's test;
			
			Note
			this section requires careful thought as far as testing goes. It can take much more time than first anticipated. The testing needs to be carefully analysed with, if necessary, structured walk-throughs used at each stage.

Figure 3.15   The Installation Procedure – Summary

of the network or systems manager should have been considered within the stage of choosing the network. These subjects outline the requirements that make the manager's end task so much easier to carry out while also relating to the applications to which the network will be put.

Security

This takes into account the following points:

— resiliency;

— recovery;

— availability;

— reliability;

— accessibility.

The resiliency of a system is a reflection of its ability to withstand failures. If, when laying down the system requirements, it is important that the system must not go 'off-the-air' should a failure occur in the master, then it may be necessary to have not one but two systems. This means that the master system is duplicated.

The duplicated system can function in a number of ways:

Cold standby: the duplicate master must be 'brought up' from a cold start before taking over the master's duties.

Hot standby: the duplicate master is immediately ready to take over the master's duties.

Hot standby + timed switchover: as the hot standby but the duplicate master only takes over the master's duties after a pre-set time.

Hot standby + load sharing: the duplicate is ready to take over *all* of the master's duties. However, while it is operating in the duplicate mode it is already carrying out some of the functions.

Synchronous operation: the system operates in a completely synchronous mode.

The period from when the master fails until the time that the system becomes fully operational again is known as the recovery period. Recovery could result from duplicating the master but it is more often the case that recovery of the system relates to putting the information from floppy disk back onto the system. This brings us to the area of taking security back-ups of software programs and correct archiving procedures.

It is the responsibility of the manager of the system to ensure that back-up copies of software are taken at pre-set intervals. The system may have to be totally taken down if a full back-up is being implemented. When choosing the system hardware the amount of down-time for backing-up procedures depends upon the medium being used for the back-up copy. To back-up a 15-Megabyte Winchester disk using floppy disks can take an excessive amount of time, depending upon the amount of software to be copied. For this reason it may be required to produce the back-ups on tape-streamer.

If and when a system does go off-the-air it is important to have a good relationship with the supplier or maintenance department. It is usually this relationship or agreement that has an effect on the mean time to repair.

The reliability, maintainability and availability are all factors that reflect the systems 'quality of service' as seen by the end users. It is perhaps useful at this stage to provide some definitions that will help to put these concepts into perspective:

Reliability: the probability that a device or system will be working after a specified time.

Maintainability: the probability that a device or system will be repaired and restored to service in less time (or equal to) the specified period of reliability.

> Availability: the probability that a device or system is functioning.

From these definitions it can be stated that:

the mean time between failures = the mean time to failure
+
the mean time to repair

and

$$\text{the availability} = \frac{\text{the mean time to failure}}{\text{the mean time between failures}}$$

It is an important aspect of the system manager's function to realise just what the above points mean and draw conclusions as to the consequences of each within his own department or organisation.

In order to maintain, or repair, an end-user's workstation it may be necessary to shut down the whole system so as to remove the workstation from the network. Clearly a network of this type is undesirable as the mean time between failures of an individual workstation directly affects the availability of the whole system!

The maintenance of a system does not stop at the hardware, software maintenance is also required.

When a system is purchased from a supplier there will undoubtedly be subsequent releases of operating system software and proprietary software. These new releases, although compatible with other versions, will contain enhancements and bug fixes. When they are incorporated into the system it is advisable to archive the old system software and store it safely with the software back-ups which are taken for security purposes. It is always possible then to revert back to the old working version should any problems be encountered with new versions.

When developing software it is important to have a predefined set of standards covering such areas as, for example, filenames, structures and format. This discipline makes the future maintenance of developed software very much easier.

If a number of networks are to be implemented and all contact with the supplier has been through a central point, then provision for a 'hot-line' for helping and dealing with enquiries from end-users must be allowed for. In addition to this it is most useful to organise a users group. This becomes more important if the network is being instigated by a central department within a large company and the users are remotely located. Not only is it possible to monitor network usage, identify training needs and respond to enquiries but it is also possible to identify the software requirements and minimise duplication.

The last point to be considered on the security side is accessibility, or the use of passwords to gain entry to the system. Operating systems with a hierarchical file structure makes the system easier to control against unauthorised access. It is essential that the file controlling the access passwords is in itself adequately protected. The whole area of security is covered in much greater detail in the references for this chapter. When considering the security side of a network it is necessary to look at the type of cable used (see Chapter 4), in addition to the password access facilities. Another potentially important candidate as a security tool is the bridge. If you recall, the bridge's function was described as linking together two similar local networks. It may be possible to limit the access to one of the networks by using the bridge as part of a security check. Sensitive data could then be kept wholly on one of the networks with only selected users on the other network having access, via the bridge.

Management Utilities

In addition to the management utilities provided by the network supplier, such as setting up hard disk partition sizes, setting up user workstations and setting up the hard disk partitions status (eg read/write, read only, etc), it is also useful to have access to good diagnostics utilities and traffic analysis utilities.

The previous section, covering installation, emphasised the importance of running self-test software on individual devices. Diagnostics utilities are used to track down where a fault has occurred so that the relevant equipment can be isolated and the fault fixed in the minimum amount of time.

The traffic analysis utility can be used to monitor network performance and quickly identify relevant weak areas. This also allows a system to be tailored to fit rather than taking the risk of overproviding equipment simply because it was not known what was required.

A summary of the operational and management requirements with emphasis on specific points to note is shown in Figure 3.16.

OPERATIONAL AND MANAGEMENT REQUIREMENT	POINTS TO NOTE
security — resiliency — recovery — availability — reliability — accessibility	back-up systems required (back to the design stage); back-up master: archiving software: software standards; does whole system need to be taken down when attaching or removing workstations? will encourage or discourage use by end-users; provision of password facilities;
consumable costs	floppy disks, paper and ribbon for printer;
maintenance — software — hardware	implement rigorous software standards for ease of future software maintenance: implement the supplier's system software updates; if a maintenance contract is taken out with the supplier is it blanket coverage or on a call-out basis? Does the hardware maintenance agreement chosen have any impact on the supply of system software updates?
hidden costs	software licensing agreements: training (does this come complete with the system package?): management time required for system operation: user groups: enquiry/help 'hot-line' for hand-holding: analysing traffic analysis (useful for future expansion needs).

Figure 3.16 Summary of Operational and Management Requirements

4 Technologies and Architectures Available

INTRODUCTION

The description and general classification of networks has already been discussed (see Chapter 1). In this chapter the focus is on the classification of local area networks (including microcomputer networks) with attention to the technologies and architectures available.

Microcomputer networks, as described previously, usually have a raw data rate transmission of less than (or equal to) 10 million bits per second. In this chapter, micronets come under the common heading of local area networks in order to discuss the following topics: transmission media, topologies and network access and sharing methods.

The three topics stated above will all combine to provide a description of a particular network. However, only the third topic (network access and sharing methods) provides the most useful classification. The reason for this is that it is the only topic which is inherent, as a system feature, in the network design.

When designing a network using the above topics as ground rules it is essential to consider the network access and sharing methods so as to produce the most cost-effective solution for the transmission media and topology to be used.

The design of any system is a constant feedback process taking into account all of the possible parameters. Networks are no different to any other system in as far as utilising basic design principles.

With these points in mind the topics mentioned above will be examined more closely.

TRANSMISSION MEDIA

The applications and requirements (see Chapters 2 and 3) must be taken into account when choosing the type of transmission media to be used for the network. Once the applications and requirements have been set out, the choice of a suitable medium is made easier. In most of the instances of networking micros, where equipment from a single supplier is used, the luxury of a choice of transmission media is not available.

The types of transmission media may be split into two categories:

> Guided – Twisted-pair cable, coaxial cable, multi-way cable, fibre optic cable

> Unguided (or free space) – Radio waves, microwave, satellite links, infra-red.

(Unguided media are covered for completeness only. The types of networks under consideration in this book will undoubtedly use guided media.)

Suppliers of systems using both guided and unguided media will quote a data rate, usually the raw data rate without the header or control information added. The header and control information is redundant data required for routeing, addressing, error checking, etc. This is explained more fully later. In order to provide a comparison between the different media types a reference chart is provided at the end of this section.

Guided Media – Twisted-Pair Cable

This type of medium was originally used in the public switched telephone network and for this reason became the main form of medium when data transmission was introduced. One or more pairs of wires are contained within a cable. Each pair of wires is twisted together (Figure 4.1) to provide an even distribution of the electrical characteristics over the whole length of the cable.

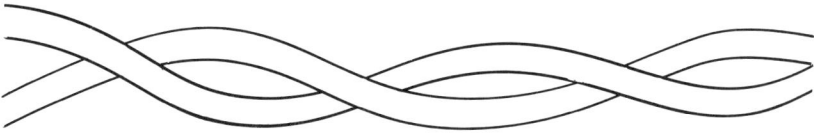

Figure 4.1   Twisted-pair Wire

Both analogue and digital signals may be transmitted over a twisted-pair cable. Signal distortion takes place during the transmission, the signal being subject to attenuation and timing irregularities (Figure 4.2). For these reasons the medium is best suited for transmission of information over relatively short distances, although repeaters may be used to amplify and regenerate the waveform.

If the transmission system parameters (ie cable quality, technique for inserting and extracting information to/from the cable) are carefully chosen there is no reason why a transmission rate of 10 million bits per second (raw data rate) should not be achieved, at least over a few hundred metres.

By using repeaters and thus utilising fully active channels the transmission distance and the transmission rate may be increased. Unfortunately, the cost also increases because of the need to purchase repeaters.

Twisted-pair cable does not lend itself very well for use as a broadcast bus, the requirements for a broadcast bus being long, distortion-free and passive. A passive channel will contain no repeaters. Reconstitution and regeneration will either clean up the signal or reform the signal (Figure 4.3).

The additional problem of using twisted-pair cable as a broadcast bus comes in the fact that it has a high electrical capacitance. This has the effect of severely distorting the signal. A solution to this problem has been known for a long time and used extensively by telephone companies transmitting speech. The solution is to load the line at set intervals with inductive coils. This does have the effect of creating a low pass filter on the line. This is clearly no problem when transmitting 4,000 Hz voice signals over the telephone network but of very little use at the higher frequency

The tails in the output pulses tend to overlap causing ISI

Output Pulse

Tails

Tails

Cable

Inter Symbol Interference (ISI)

Input Pulse

Variation in set logic levels

Noise

Variation in the timing of the leading and trailing edges

Jitter

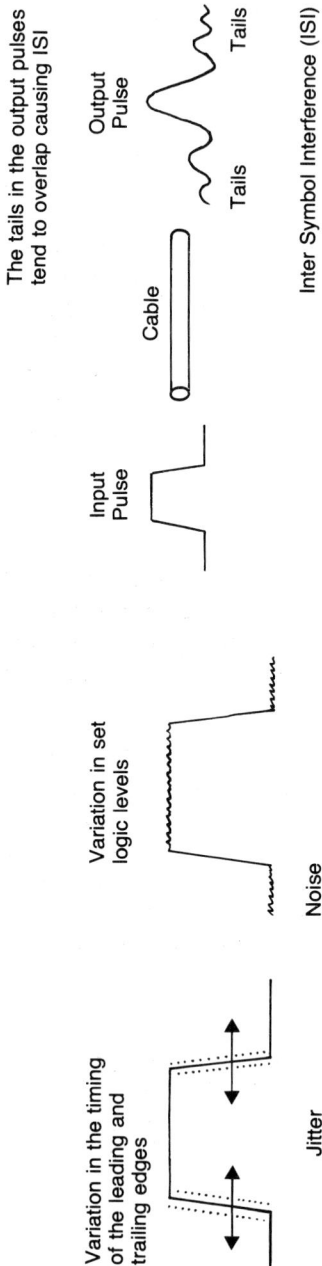

Figure 4.2   Examples of Signal Distortion

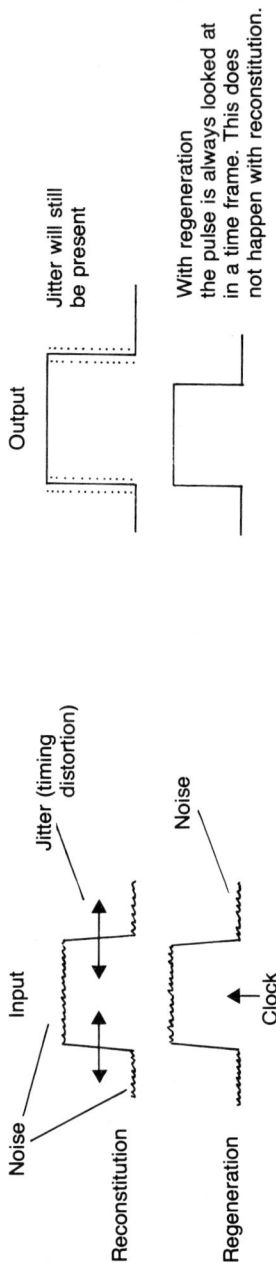

Output

Jitter will still be present

With regeneration the pulse is always looked at in a time frame. This does not happen with reconstitution.

Jitter (timing distortion)

Input

Noise

Noise

Reconstitution

Regeneration

Clock

Figure 4.3   Reconstitution and Regeneration of Signals

requirement of local area networks. Lumped loading on a transmission line also attenuates the signal and slows down the velocity of propagation and hence the data rate. You do not get anything for nothing!

If a twisted-pair cable has been 'tuned' to get the best results then tapping into it will upset this. The tuning of the cable/system will have to be performed again. This tuning may well include balancing the lines in order to counter the effects of the cable emitting radiation which tends to make the data transmitted on the link available to eavesdroppers with suitable equipment. Shielding can also be provided on the cable, at extra cost, in order to reduce the electromagnetic radiation emissions. Unfortunately unshielded twisted-pair cable is also susceptible to external interference and for this reason should not be used in electrically noisy environments.

Multi-way Cable

This type of cable comes in the form of flat ribbon cable or round multi-core cable. It is easy to install but unfortunately it attenuates the signal and is susceptible to external electromagnetic interference. The plus point, however, is that the data and control lines can be separate making interfacing so much easier.

The individual wires within the cable may now be used for data (either serial or parallel), or used to signify a bus 'busy' signal or used to implement clock or synchronisation signals. This latter use of one of the wires for synchronisation signals removes the requirement to encode the data to be transmitted in such a way as to provide synchronisation within the pulse train. Further information on encoding data is provided in the last section of this chapter.

Figure 4.4 shows examples of multi-way cable.

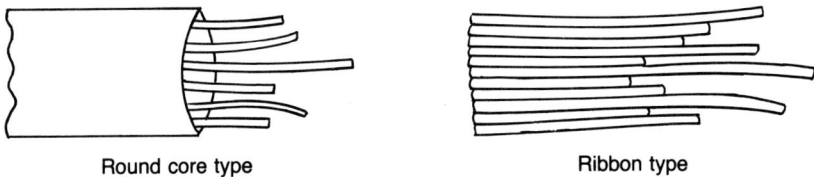

Round core type   Ribbon type

Figure 4.4   Multi-way Cable

Coaxial Cable

This type of cable is made up from a single central conductor surrounded by a dielectric material such as PVC, which is in turn surrounded by a sleeve of copper wire mesh or extruded aluminium. This assembly is then surrounded by a protective outer sleeve. An example of the layers that make up a coaxial cable is shown in Figure 4.5.

Coaxial cable is subject to a phenomenon known as the 'skin effect'. This takes place at high frequencies and is simply induced current concentrating on the outside of the conductor. Although this has a tendency to increase the cable resistance and hence the attenuation it does reduce the crosstalk (the effect of one cable's signal affecting another in close proximity). The reduction in crosstalk comes about because the cable's own signal does not radiate outside nor does induced current penetrate the cable. Very high data rates using both digital and analogue transmission techniques are possible using coaxial cable. Coaxial cable is typically used at transmission rates greater than sixty thousand bits per second.

The reduction in crosstalk also proves very useful from the security aspect, at least for broadband signals operating at high frequency. If no signals radiate outside the cable then it is impossible to eavesdrop with listening equipment (as was possible with the other cable types).

Coaxial cable has been used in television, radio and other high frequency applications for many years and is a well tried medium. The cable television industry produced a requirement for

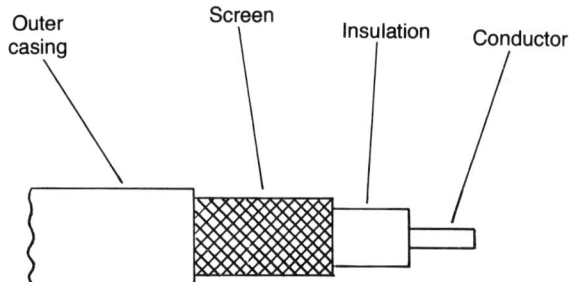

Figure 4.5   Coaxial Cable

peripheral equipment to support this transmission media. That equipment is now available 'off the shelf'.

The cable is available in two types. The essential difference is the characteristic impedance. The characteristic impedance (and the velocity of wave propagation ie data rate) are independent of frequency at high frequencies resulting in the fact that the line (or transmission bus) can be correctly terminated with a resistance, typically 50 ohms or 75 ohms. These terminations reduce the effects of echoes and reflections. In baseband systems the line does not have to be 'tuned' when new equipment is added because the characteristics have not changed.

Baseband systems do not operate at high frequencies and use a passive medium for transmission and, as was explained above, will accept additional equipment on the bus very easily. This ease of tapping the line can be a security problem as can the fact that because baseband does not use modulation it is much easier to eavesdrop by picking up radiated signals.

The last section in this chapter describes the various network access and sharing methods employed by suppliers' systems. It is in effect these which limit the length of a cable.

The cost of coaxial cable is higher than twisted-pair but it is easier to connect to and does provide some security from eaves-droppers listening close by. However, because the cable is made up of several layers of material it is less flexible and thus harder to install.

Optical Transmission Systems

This type of transmission system is available from a number of suppliers and transmits light rather than electrical signals. The fibre comes in three types: mono-mode, multi-mode step index and multi-mode graded index. The index refers to the refractive index of the glass used. The basic system design for an optical fibre transmission system can be represented by the block schematic diagram shown in Figure 4.6.

A detailed analysis of an optical fibre transmission system would require mathematical analysis of source and detector performances, including, in the case of the detector, analysis of noise (quantum noise, dark current shot noise, thermal noise, post detection amplifier noise and avalanche noise). This information is of more use to an optical fibre transmission system designer. The reader should note the reference for further information. Here the aim is to promote an awareness of the equipment used for sources and detectors and a description of the optical fibre types. Even though this type of system transmits light instead of electrical impulses there are certain similarities with its electrical counterpart, as well as certain deficiencies. The optical transmission systems designer can mix and match sources, detectors and optical transmission media just as can his electrical counterpart.

Sources

The sources used to get the light into the cable usually come in the

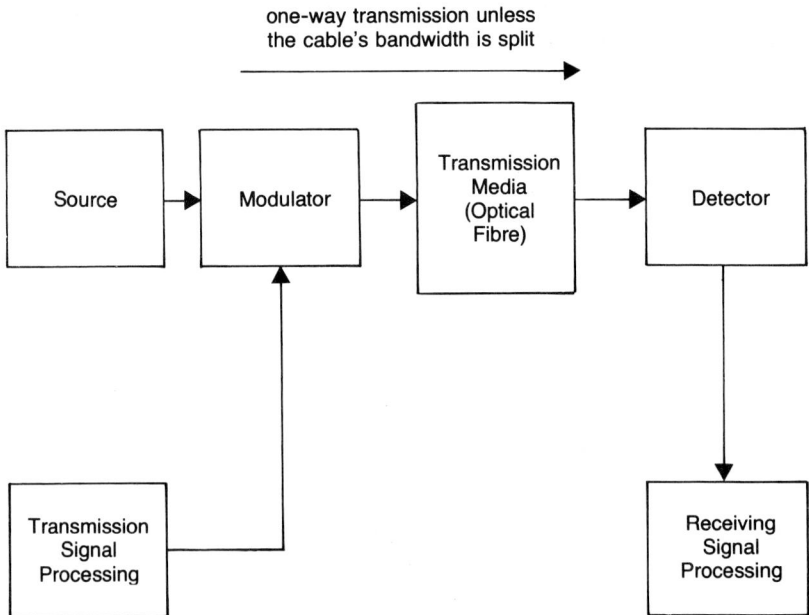

Figure 4.6   Optical Fibre Transmission System

form of either a LED (light emitting diode) or a LASER diode (semiconductor type).

The LED is suitable for use with multi-mode fibres. The reason for this is that the light emitted is not limited to a selected wavelength. The actual LED usually comes with a short length of fibre already attached (see Figure 4.7).

The fibre comes attached to the LED because of the problems associated with jointing typical fibres and ensuring that all of the light offered to the fibre actually goes in.

The LASER diode source, on the other hand, offers a very narrow line width and is commonly used with mono-mode fibres. The light emission comes from the edge rather than the surface, as in LEDs (Figure 4.8).

The problem of getting all of the light that comes out of the LASER into the fibre is still present. The method for doing this by using a concentrating fibre lens is shown in Figure 4.9. The assembly is mounted on thick film.

Detectors

The detectors used are usually PIN photo-diodes or avalanche photo-diodes. Each of these detectors has its own advantages

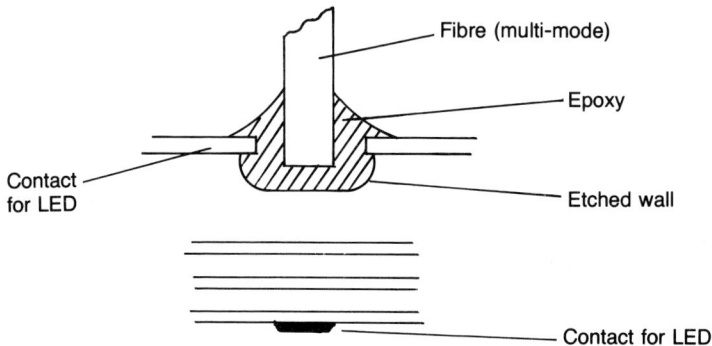

Figure 4.7 Typical LED

and disadvantages. These are of most use to the optical transmission systems designer. They are described very briefly below.

PIN Photo-diode

The 'I' in PIN is the important part. It stands for INTRINSIC. This intrinsic region in the PIN photo-diode is more sensitive to light falling on it hence the region is made wide. The devices themselves can handle data rates in the gigabit region.

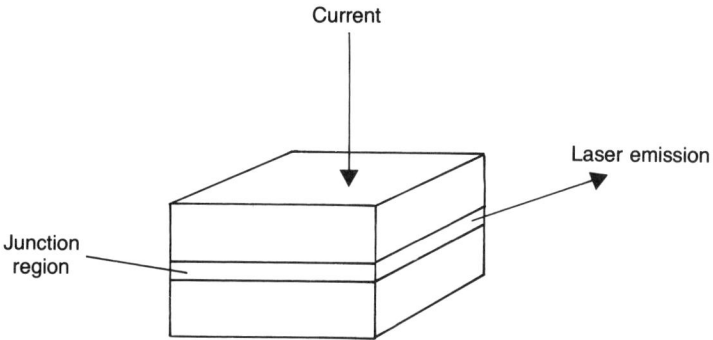

Figure 4.8   Semiconductor LASER

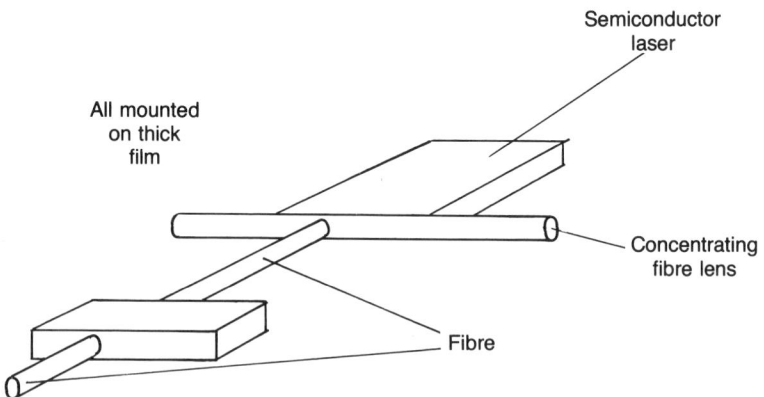

Figure 4.9   Coupling a LASER to the Fibre

Avalanche Photo-diode

The avalanche description is just what it means, ie for a small amount of light falling on the detector the resultant output is quite large. This provides the avalanche gain. Unfortunately avalanches in real life tend to be unpredictable. In this respect the avalanche photo-diode is no different and this random gain mechanism introduces its own noise problems. The avalanche gain is also very temperature dependent.

Optical Fibre

The three types of fibre available are shown in Figure 4.10.

Mono-mode Fibres

This type of fibre has a very narrow central core making jointing very difficult. However, the wavelengths of light transmitted are more selective and so higher data transmission rates can be used.

Multi-mode Step Index

This is very similar to the mono-mode fibre in that the fibre contains a central core. This core is much wider than in the mono-mode case and thus the light is prone to dispersion effects. The wider central core does make it easier to joint.

Multi-mode Graded Index

The central core of this fibre has a refractive index that varies with the radius of the fibre. The benefit of this is that the light rays propagating down the fibre tend to reach the end at the same time. The fibre has a self-focusing property. An additional attraction to this type of fibre is that it is easy to joint.

Very good quality fibres result in 0.5 dB/km loss. This is just scattering with none of the associated higher frequency losses you get with coaxial cable.

The low-loss nature of this medium makes distances of 100 km possible between repeaters, although when repeaters are used the light must be translated into electrical impulses before amplification and then back into light for subsequent retransmission. This can make long links quite expensive.

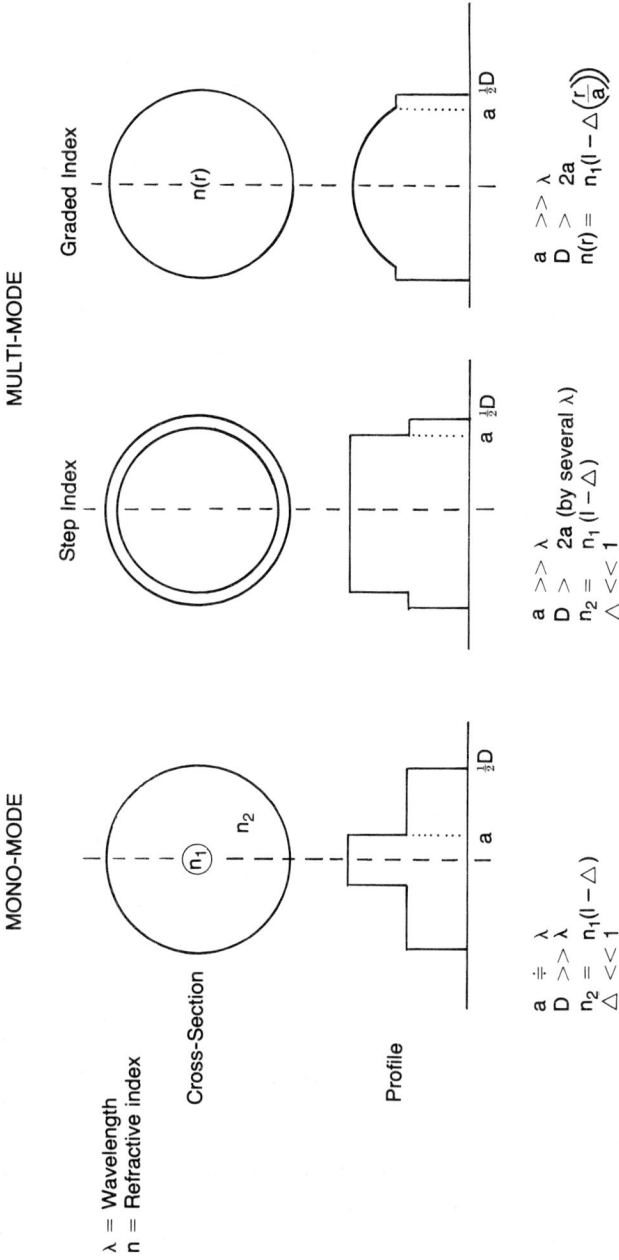

Figure 4.10   Optical Fibre Types

Optical fibres are also immune to electromagnetic radiation making them very useful in noisy environments. The information carried by the fibres does not radiate outside the medium hence the data carried is more secure from eavesdroppers.

Tapping into the fibre is difficult so they are more suited for use in loop and ring topologies rather than broadcast bus systems.

Unguided Media

These are mentioned only to complete the picture. In general the cost restriction excludes this type of media from being used to link micros. However, the microcomputer networks may be indirectly linked to other networks using this media. If so, then the unguided media solution would be used because it formed part of the solution for a larger local area network concept.

The possibilities for unguided media are:

— radio;

— microwave;

— infra red;

— satellite communications;

— laser.

The summary table (Figure 4.11) shows the advantages and disadvantages of the types of transmission media discussed in this section and highlights key points. Unguided media are not shown in the summary table because at present there are few available.

TOPOLOGIES

The topology of the network defines the way in which the nodes in the network are interconnected. When defining a network topology consideration must be given to rationalising the interconnections in order to provide an economical number with which the network will still function. For example, if all of the nodes were interconnected in a mesh (Figure 4.12) and each node contained routeing intelligence then, if a link was down to an adjacent node, there would still be (N-2) routes available to that adjacent node via an intermediate node.

Transmission Media	Advantages	Disadvantages
Twisted Pair Cable	readily available; tried, tested and well understood medium; best suited for point-to-point links; low cost; easy to install; will transmit digital and analogue information	extra devices needed for high speed data transmission adds to cost; radiates to its environment when transmitting data making it not very secure from eavesdroppers – requires shielding; if cable has been 'tuned' then expansion is not as easy as just adding an extra device – cable must be 're-tuned'; high attenuation of signal; cannot be used in electrically noisy environments if unshielded
Multi-way Cable	readily available; tried, tested and well understood medium; suited to baseband ring or bus systems; easy to install; control and data lines can be split making interfacing very easy; parallel data transmission possible	radiates to its environment when transmitting data making it not very secure from eavesdroppers – requires shielding; high attenuation of signal; cannot be used in electrically noisy environments; more expensive than twisted pair or ordinary coaxial cable
Coaxial Cable	available as baseband or broadband; well understood medium; ancillary equipment readily available and presently used in cable TV industry; easy to connect new equipment to baseband cable; signals do not radiate outside cable; shielded and secure from external electromagnetic interference; high bit rate transmission possible; cable TV coaxial is cheap and readily available; ideal for broadcast network; good geographic coverage	better quality cable for broadband transmissions can be expensive; better quality cable can be difficult to install; ease of tapping the line to connect new equipment can be a security problem; easier to eavesdrop on baseband systems

Figure 4.11   Summary of Transmission Media: Advantages vs Disadvantages

Transmission Media	Advantages	Disadvantages
Optical Fibre	less dispersion effects because of the selective wavelengths used (mono-mode); high data transmission rates (large bandwidth); very secure from outside interference; light does not propagate outside the medium; suited to ring and loop technologies; physically small; very low loss; multi-mode graded index provides an auto focus for the light, most systems use this type of fibre; increasing interest in mono-mode fibres	jointing difficulties because of narrow central core (mono-mode); can only use laser diode source for mono-mode; repeaters must convert to electrical signals, ie optical [electrical (re-generate) electrical]; optical single fibre is one way transmission (although the bandwidth can be split for transmit and receive channels); multi-mode step index is more prone to dispersion effects; cost is still relatively high

Figure 4.11   Summary of Transmission Media: Advantages vs Disadvantages (Continued)

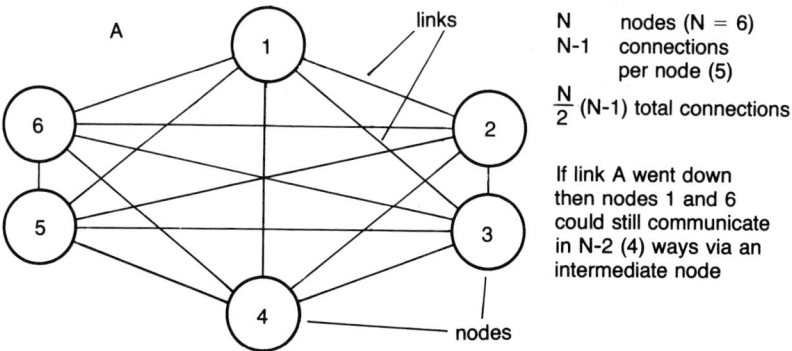

N   nodes (N = 6)
N-1   connections per node (5)
$\frac{N}{2}$ (N-1) total connections

If link A went down then nodes 1 and 6 could still communicate in N-2 (4) ways via an intermediate node

Figure 4.12   Mesh Network

Mesh networks may be used for instances of high traffic conditions in order to provide alternate routes and thus traffic sharing. They are utilised in high security applications. Because of the obvious redundancy at work in this topology of network it is not a candidate for local area network use. The reason for this is that local area networks are designed to provide common access to shared resources at low cost. The cost of a fully interconnected mesh network is high because of the amount of cabling required and the intelligence required in the nodes in order to provide routeing.

The topologies found in local area networks usually come in the form of a star, loop, ring or bus.

Star

The topology of a star network is shown in Figure 4.13. A typical star network is that of a PABX (see Chapter 7).

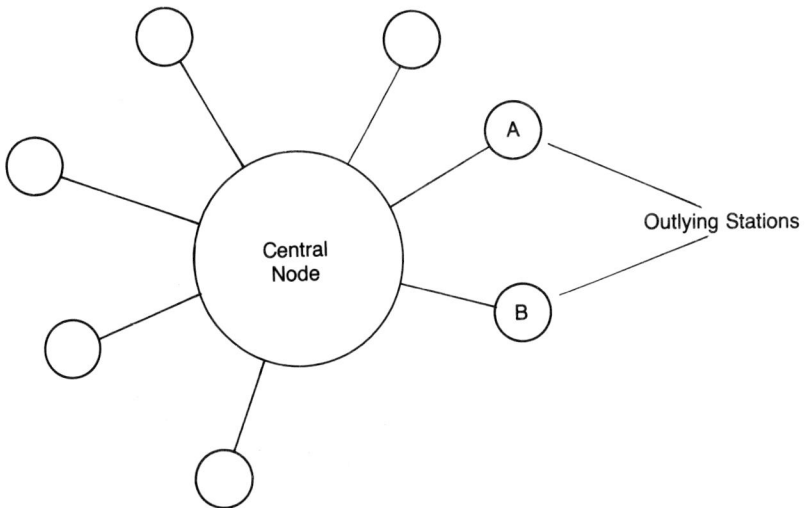

Figure 4.13   Star Network

The central node usually employs switching techniques to interconnect the outlying stations. The benefit is that all of the intelligence can be in the central node. Broadcast facilities are usually not found on this type of network as only direct interconnection between A and B (via the central node) is possible at any one time.

The security of this system also leaves a lot to be desired. If the central node goes down then the whole system is out of action.

For these reasons a central node star system in itself employing pure and simple switching is not used for a local area network. However, it does provide an important module to be used in local

Loop

A loop network topology (Figure 4.14) uses an intelligent controller through which all messages are routed. The route of a message going from A to B is shown.

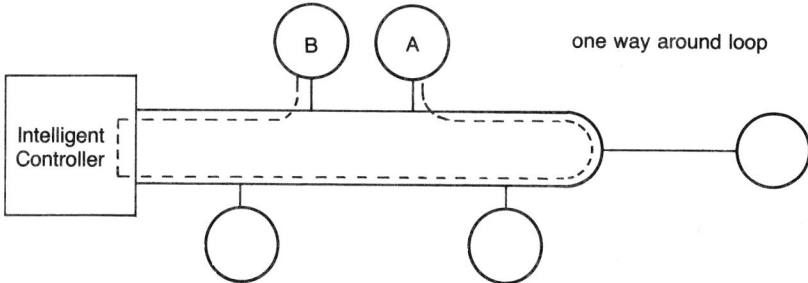

Figure 4.14   Loop Network

The intelligent controller may choose to send an empty packet around the loop, which, when coming to a node wishing to use it will be filled and sent to its destination or may choose simply to poll each node in turn.

If the intelligent controller goes down then data transmission around the loop is effectively stopped.

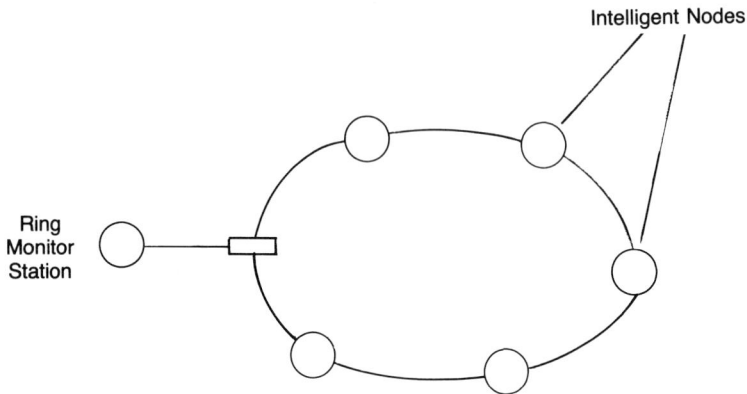

Figure 4.15   Ring Network

Ring

Although like a loop in appearance, the ring (Figure 4.15) differs from it considerably.

The intelligent central controller described in the previous topologies no longer exists. Instead of the intelligence being centred in this controller it is now spread out throughout the nodes, each having an equal amount of intelligence.

There is, however, a ring monitor station connected to the ring whose purpose it is to monitor the ring and remove unwanted or corrupted packets, start up the ring and provide a graceful shut down.

The direction of data flow around the ring is usually one way. However, some manufacturers' proprietary networks are reconfigurable in the instance of a link failure.

Bus or Highway

Unlike the ring, the data bus (Figure 4.16) is a passive network. The peripherals hang on the bus listening for data packets with their address. If no information is being transported on the bus then the network is completely quiet. The access methods are very important in order to make efficient use of the network.

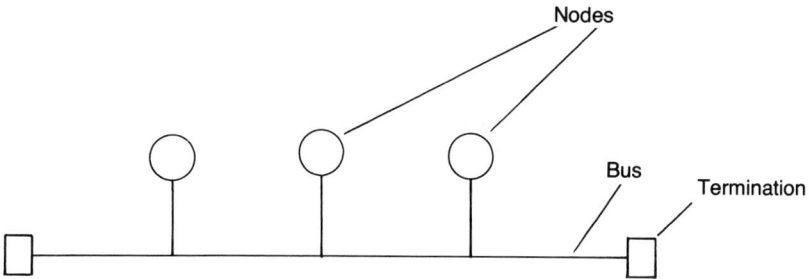

Figure 4.16 Bus or Highway Network

When a node wishes to transmit data to another node it must listen to the bus to see if anyone else is transmitting. If no data is on the bus then it will transmit. The nodes must be intelligent enough to listen to the bus and recognise their own addresses in order to receive incoming data. The topologies are summarised (Figure 4.17). This table lists the advantages and disadvantages of each type of topology.

NETWORK ACCESS AND SHARING METHODS

At the beginning of this chapter it was pointed out that network access and sharing methods provide the most useful classification for a system. This statement can now be explored.

In general the transmission media used for a network can be of any type mentioned in this chapter. With the progress in technical research and applications it is increasingly probable that the newer techniques (eg optical fibre) will be used more and more for both new and existing systems.

The topology of a system is not a true description. A ring system may look like a star and a bus system can have a tree configuration (Figure 4.18).

The description of access and sharing techniques now follows an initial explanation of the terms 'Baseband', 'Broadband' and a brief introduction into Manchester encoding techniques used in baseband signalling.

Topology	Advantages	Disadvantages
Star	central node contains intelligence hence cheap peripheral nodes; easy to attach new devices without disturbing the system; very good for interconnecting systems; the centre of the star can provide circuit, message (store and forward) or packet switching; readily available networks in the form of suitable PABXs	system crashes if central node fails; communications port limitations in central node (max. devices determined by number of ports); central node should be at the physical centre to optimize cable running; central node is the shared resource not the transmission medium as in the case of a local area network; dedicated point-to-point connections; usually no broadcast facility
Loop	broadcast facility available; central node contains intelligence hence cheap peripheral nodes if polling is implemented	if loop controller fails then the system fails; low speed transmission is usually implemented, restricting data throughput
Ring	no central node hence no dependence; high speed data transmission is possible; implementation can be cheap and easy to control overall; usually used in a deterministic system in that every node gets an equal chance to transmit; nodes can be given a priority	a break in the ring stops the system, although certain proprietary systems are reconfigurable; more intelligence required in the nodes, hence nodes are relatively more expensive; system must be taken down to add in a new node; monitor station required to monitor ring and remove corrupted packets
Bus or Highway	no central node; usually used in a probabalistic system (eg CSMA/CD); implementation can be easy to install); a break in the bus, isolating *one* user may not affect the whole system; many proprietary systems use 'standard' access techniques eg CSMA/CD; can use different forms of access techniques besides CSMA/CD, eg POLL etc, easily expandable	intelligence required in the nodes, hence nodes are relatively more expensive; break in the bus not affecting the whole system is dependent upon the proprietary system. Some systems may require a clock module to be present on the bus; data throughput may degrade under heavy usage

Figure 4.17   Topology Comparison Table

Baseband

This type of signalling is simple and in common use in many local area networks. The term baseband means that it contains no form of modulation at all. The data does, however, require sufficient transitions in the transmitted pulse train in order for the receiving terminal to keep in synchronisation for asynchronous transmission. The transitions in effect provide a clock.

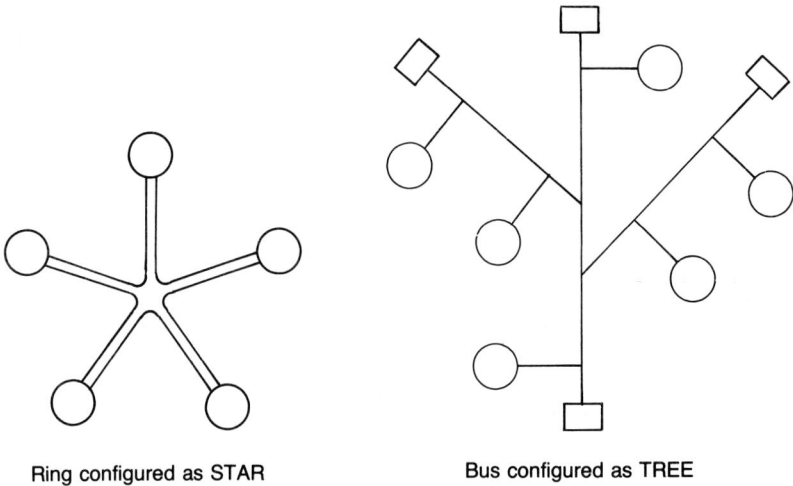

Ring configured as STAR   Bus configured as TREE

Figure 4.18   Network Configurations

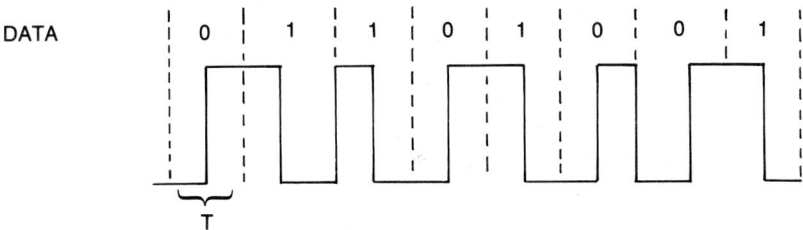

a transition occurs at the centre of every time slot (T)

Figure 4.19   Manchester Encoding

Methods of encoding the data in order to provide sufficient transitions are used in Walsh, Miller and Bipolar techniques of coding (Pritchard, 1979). The most common one in use however is that of Manchester Encoding, Figure 4.19.

The cables used for baseband systems tend to attenuate the signal. For this reason baseband systems are usually used over short distances. When used over longer distances the signal is usually modulated onto a carrier. The baseband system thus has one signal at a time on the transmission medium.

Transmission over longer distances may also use Broadband.

Broadband

The method frequency multiplexes several users onto a single cable. By definition the bandwidth of the transmission medium must be wider in order that several users can be assigned their frequency slot or channel. For example, if a broadband system has a bandwidth of 300 MHz (300 million cycles per second) and if the speech band of 300 Hz – 3400 Hz is rationalised to a band of 4000 Hz then 75,000 telephone channels could be created. The split has no need to be of this form, clearly a whole section of the available bandwidth could be utilised for data transmission. Broadband systems had their origin in the cable TV industry.

Broadband systems use a one- or two-cable implementation to link all of the nodes on the network. The two-cable implementation (Figure 4.20) uses one cable to transmit and one cable to receive. The cables run side by side and are terminated by a special receiver/transmitter called the HEADEND. Each node is attached to the cable through a radio frequency (RF) transmitter/receiver modem.

The one-cable system splits the available bandwidth of the single cable into two separate bands. One band is used for transmitting and the other for receiving with the HEADEND providing the translation. The system is outlined in Figure 4.21.

Full-duplex operation is possible with broadband systems because of the separate frequencies used for transmitting and receiving. An overview is now given of methods of gaining access to and sharing the network's transmission medium.

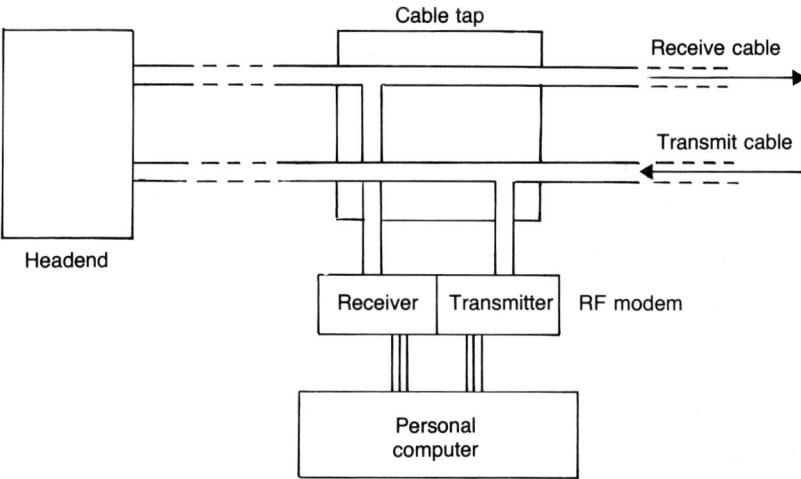

Figure 4.20   The Two-Cable Broadband System

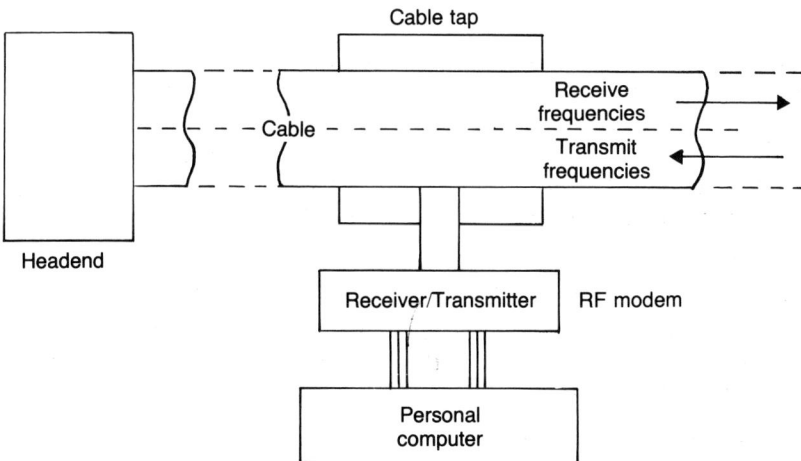

Figure 4.21   The One-Cable Broadband System

Frequency Division Multiplexing

Medium resource sharing using frequency division multiplexing of fdm techniques means that the bandwidth is split up into discrete frequency bands and these bands are then used as the transmission channels. The technique is shown in Figure 4.22.

If the available bandwidth of the system is $f_{12} - f_1$, then channel C1 is allocated the frequency band starting at f_1, and ending at f_2.

It should be noted that the overall bandwidth of a system is limited by the bandwidth of the worst component. The components could be any part of the system, from the transmission medium itself, to the end-user terminals.

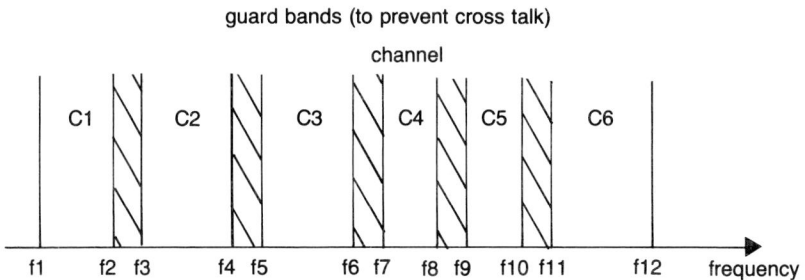

Figure 4.22   fdm Resource Sharing

Time Division Multiplexing

This method of sharing a resource (Figure 4.23) is based on the fact that the transmission medium is operating as a single channel but the channel is shared out in time.

The data is put onto the channel in a strict sequence coinciding with the time slot allocation.

Polling

This method of sharing requires a master node to ask other nodes on the network if they have any data they would like to transmit. There is a strict sequence of operation for this type of technique,

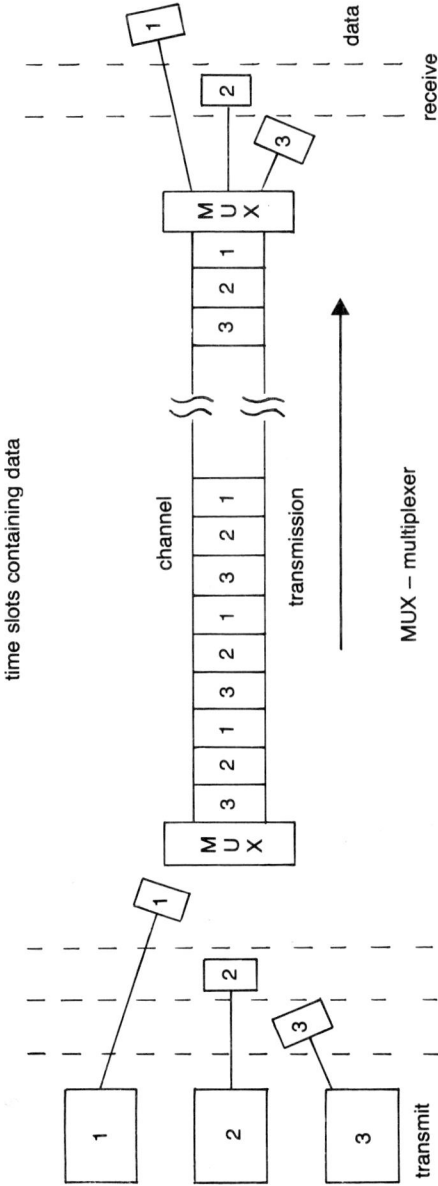

Figure 4.23   tdm Resource Sharing

although a priority system (a system whereby a heavily used node gets more access to the network) may be set up.

Broadcast Bus

Using this type of technique every node on the network must listen to the bus in order to identify any messages destined for itself. The recognition of the correct message for the correct node is based upon an address of the relevant node being contained in the message itself.

Token Passing

This is an actual technique (Figure 4.24) used on a broadcast bus or a ring system in order to ensure that a node gains control of the bus/ring. The sequence of passing the token may not necessarily follow from node to node. A priority may be set up so that one particular (high priority) node gets the token more often than the others.

From Figure 4.24 it can be seen that, during any one cycle of token passing, nodes 2 and 3 are of equal priority, node 1 is high priority and node 4 is low priority. Transmission of data onto the bus may only take place when the node is in possession of the token.

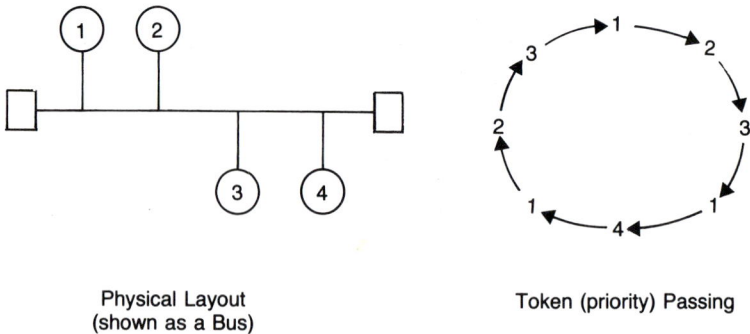

Physical Layout
(shown as a Bus)

Token (priority) Passing

Figure 4.24   Token Passing

Carrier Sense Multiple Access with Collision Detection (CSMA/CD)

With the CSMA/CD technique the node listens to the bus and if it is not in use transmits its message. If, between the time of listening and the time of transmission another node gains access, and a collision of data occurs on the bus, it is detected and all nodes back off. The sequence by which the nodes then try to regain access to the bus can be varied so that all nodes do not attempt to retransmit at the same time and so get locked into a sequence of collision-retransmission-collision, etc. This contention (for the bus) technique is commonly used in systems and is the basis of ETHERNET.

If the bus utilisation is high then the performance of this type of system can drop off quite sharply. This is because a node, when trying to gain access to the bus will find it busy and so back off and then retry.

Carrier Sense Multiple Access with Collision Avoidance (CSMA/CA)

CSMA/CA is a combination of normal slotted time division multiplexing and CSMA/CD.

The system is split up into allocated time slots for each node to transmit its information. If any node is unready to transmit then that time slot remains unused. If all of the nodes are unready and have been given the chance to transmit once then the system reverts to the CSMA/CD mode of operation. Once the channel has been used again to transmit information, the system switches back to the time slot method of operation.

Fixed Slot

Used in ring systems and formed from a basis of tdm. When a node wishes to transmit data it must wait until the slot allocated to it comes around. It may then insert its message.

Empty Slot

This technique uses a system that employs a number of empty packets circulating around the ring. When a node wishes to transmit data it waits for the empty packet to come around, inserts its

Access or Sharing Technique	Advantages	Disadvantages
Frequency Division Multiplexing (FDM)	overall bandwidth can be split into several dedicated channels (less than or equal to the total bandwidth); the whole bandwidth can be utilised if necessary; equipment is readily available; individual channel(s) could be used for a real-time application	channels require guard bands to minimise the effects of crosstalk); modems must be used at the appropriate channel frequency
Time Division Multiplexing (TDM)	each terminal has a pre-allocated time slot; a good way of fully utilising a system with limited bandwidth – every time slot has access to the whole bandwidth for a specific duration	single channel, shared in time; time slot duration and number of time slots (ie connections) limits the suitability of the method for real-time applications. Can be used in practice
Polling	each device can have exclusive use of the controller; priorities can be set up. These must be set up carefully so as not to loose the advantage of sharing the controller effectively	mainly associated with low usage terminals; not really for use in real-time control applications. The frequency of polling would have to be increased to an often unacceptable level (possibly twice the frequency of the real-time applications control rate)
Broadcast Bus	a high degree of efficiency is achieved in practice	only one user can send information at a time
Token Passing	every node gets a fair chance to transmit; 'priorities' can be set up; no limit to packet size	not really for use in real-time situations; detection of lost/corrupt packets is essential (monitor station); fairly complex to implement

Figure 4.25   Advantages and Disadvantages of Various Access and Sharing Techniques

Access or Sharing Technique	Advantages	Disadvantages
CSMA/CD	makes good use of medium; easy to implement; good for 'bursty' traffic; ETHERNET uses this technique (chip sets are available) ETHERNET implementations need not be expensive once chip sets are widely available	performance may drop off under very high utilisation; access times cannot be guaranteed; no use for synchronous data transmission, voice traffic, video
CSMA/CA	claimed to be very efficient where some nodes need more access to the system and where the overall loading is fairly high	requires more intelligence in nodes hence more expensive nodes are required
Fixed Slot	as TDM (it uses this technique)	as TDM (it uses this technique)
Empty Slot	nodes have a fair share of bandwidth; performs well under heavy loads; inexpensive; Cambridge Ring is an implementation using this technique	monitor station is needed; reliability is dependent on monitor, repeater and ring segments (reliable in practice)

Figure 4.25   Advantages and Disadvantages of Various Access and Sharing Techniques (Continued)

data, marks the packet as used and sends it on its way. It is used as the basis of the Cambridge Ring.

A protocol ensures that if the receiving node is not functioning then the sending node knows that the data has not been read. The monitor station on the ring starts the ring up from cold, gracefully closes it down, and also removes corrupted packets.

Figure 4.25 lists the advantages and disadvantages of the various access and sharing techniques.

The bus or ring is basically either shared in space or shared in time. The manufacturers' systems merely use various access techniques in order to take full advantage of the resource. At the moment the choice is between ring, bus and polled systems. The majority of manufacturers have opted for the first two techniques. However, there are successful implementations available of polled or multi-drop systems. Of these techniques fibre optics is only really practical on ring systems. In addition the only truely reconfigurable networks (when the cable has been accidentally damaged) are available on a ring. This, however, is not an inherent part of the topology and must be engineered in, making the system more expensive.

Finally it is important to mention the effects of transmission delay on a system's access technique (eg suitability for real-time applications, Figure 4.25).

The size of the packets used on the system depends on the amount of data contained in the packet in proportion to the header and trailer information, in addition to the length that can be successfully transmitted and the amount of time required to put a packet on the network.

5 Standards

WHY THE NEED?

The worlds of data communications and voice communications are growing ever closer together.

The present telecommunications network has, what is now a well defined set of so called 'standards'. These 'standards' are really only recommendations laid down by the CCITT (Consultative Commitée Internationale Telephonique et Telegraphique). They cover such areas as services and facilities, interfaces, transmission, signalling and switching, network aspects, maintenance and administrative arrangements. Although only recommendations, by adhering to these, a manufacturer of telecommunications equipment opens up his market for selling his products. The telecommunications network is ensured of interconnectivity and compatibility on a worldwide basis. A certain number of interfaces between different equipment is still required but this is now kept down to a minimum.

One of the main reasons why interfaces are still required is that manufacturers have high investment in their own equipment design and clearly are not willing to re-design.

The implementation of standards, or recommendations, by an external body (as suppliers must have a lot of influence to make their product a standard) follows four stages:

The identification, by the manufacturer, of a market used

Design of equipment, by the manufacturer, to fulfil the need

Entrance of other manufacturers into the market place

Development of standards (sometimes in parallel with the entrance of other manufacturers into the market place)

In general, standards appear when the equipment is already in the market place and can be greatly influenced by the presence of a manufacturer's proprietary equipment.

The telecommunications network was originally designed to transmit voice traffic. The range of frequencies in the voice (except for exceptional circumstances) varies from 300Hz to 3400Hz and so the network design was based around this.

The data, transmitted over this network, had to be transmitted with this limiting factor in mind. In the 1960s DATEL was introduced to transmit the data over the telephone network. The DATEL service used MODEMS (modulators/demodulators) to conform to the network requirements (ie staying within the 300Hz to 3400Hz pass band), and followed CCITT recommendations for the implementation. The connection of remote computers and terminals over a wide area network – in this case, the telephone network – had thus come about.

The frequency limitations imposed by the telephone network restricted the transmission of data, although implementations such as phase quadrature modulation (Lindsey and Simon, 1973) were introduced to increase the bit rate over leased telephone lines. The requirement thus arose for a public data network, and with it the chance to build on the standards which had evolved from the transmission of data over the telephone network.

PROPRIETARY ARCHITECTURES

The interconnection of different manufacturers computer equipment provides problems only if the same software and communications design criteria are not adhered to by all manufacturers. This is inevitably the case where designs have taken place with no liaison between any of the manufacturers. The traditional computer systems were closed: terminals, peripherals and other equipment would only connect to the equipment of a specific manufacturer. This situation is acceptable providing that the organisation only needs to use the equipment and devices within its own structure, never needing to go outside and hence running the risk of trying to connect to devices which are not compatible. Because of the range of computer equipment, office and industrial devices being put onto the market and the requirement to interconnect these, a closed network philosophy can restrict a company's expansion.

The International Standards Organisation's Reference Model of Open Systems Interconnection (OSI) provides a basis to ensure that a network of computer-based equipment from a number of different suppliers can be successfully put together. The aims of the local area network designer are the same. Because of this, local networking standards are being aligned with those of the Open Systems Interconnection.

OPEN SYSTEMS INTERCONNECTION

The layered structure which is to provide the basis by which two end-users may communicate can be seen in Figure 5.1. The objective here is to provide a simple explanation of the Open Systems

Level	Layer
7	Application layer
6	Presentation layer
5	Session layer
4	Transport layer
3	Network layer
2	Data link layer
1	Physical layer

Figure 5.1   The Layered Structure

Interconnection philosophy by looking at a layered network architecture.

The whole point of transmitting data is so that two (or more) end-users may act on the information held within the data and participate in a conversation. The end-users should not be aware of the actual mechanism used to transport the data.

The analogy is with that of an Englishman (who speaks no other language) communicating with a Frenchman (who speaks no other language). Providing that an interpreter is provided and protocols are set out such that each speaks only through the interpreter then communication between the Englishman and the Frenchman may be set up. This provides sufficient transparency such that the characteristics not really relevant to the conversation itself, ie the interpreter and the protocols, become transparent to each end-user.

Application Layer

The application packages (ie services to the end-user), where the processing of information contained within the data transmission takes place, reside in the top-most layer. This is called the Application Layer. The shielding of these end-users from inherent differences is provided by a functional layer called the Presentation Layer.

Presentation Layer

The Presentation Layer also provides the following specific functions in the case of a network, in addition to those provided by the translator in the analogy above:

— Presentation of the data in a message:

  — code conversion;

  — compression/expansion of redundant data;

  — use of standard layouts for display terminals and/or printers.

— Remote file access, either at record level or file transfer level;

— The virtual terminal concept. This is terminal emulation, set up when communication is established. The Presentation Layer at the other end translates the data to the specific device control and configuration of its end-user.

At the present the last two points are in the Applications Layer and use other services in the Presentation Layer. The Presentation Layer enables the end-users to be as independent of each other's characteristics as possible, allowing mixed suppliers to be used in a network. They can now concentrate on the conversation itself.

Session Layer

The Session Layer is responsible for establishing the relation between two end-users. Both session partners are only aware of the other partner in the session. At this level it is also specified how end-users are identified *ie* naming and/or addressing schemes (in complete systems), and ensured that the session is orderly. The Session Layer should:

— check the sequence of the messages in case delivery and sequence are not guaranted in the lower levels;

— relate messages and the responses to them, eg sequence numbers (send and receive);

— control the rules for the dialogue during the conversation.

The Session Layer does know the identity of the partner in the conversation and co-ordinates the message flow between both partners. However, it does not know where the partner is situated in the network. The next layer down, the Transport Layer creates a 'transport tube' between the end-users using the transport mechanisms in the network.

Transport Layer

The 'transport tube' introduced above is analogous to household plumbing. The waste water in a house eventually gets into the main sewer, ie where. The exact path of how it gets there is not relevant. Important functions that can be located in the Transport Layer are:

— applying flow control to the packet stream on the transport connection. The flow control is end-to-end;

— the Transport Layer provides end-system to end-system control over transmission. This occurs with complete independence of network type;

— the Session Layer tells the Transport Layer the quality of service required for the data exchange. The Transport Layer achieves this using whatever network and facilities required;

— the Transport Layer tries to shield the user from network idiosyncrasies.

The Session Layer need not be aware of the particular technique used in the transport system. The end-users exchange complete messages, the length of which is agreed between the end-users and it is not affected by considerations about the mechanisms used in between. The next lower layer, the Network Layer, routes individual messages through the actual topology of the network. The messages at this level are called packets. Messages are mapped by the Transport Layer into these packets.

The Transport Layer also provides flow control, rather like a combination of traffic lights at a busy road junction and one of those yellow boxes acting as the network, which you do not enter unless the exit is clear. Even though you have been given the go-ahead (green light) to transmit yourself across the network (yellow box), you may only proceed if your exit on the other side is ready to receive you. There may exist a need for strong interaction between the Transport Layer and the Network Layer to avoid congestion (build-up of packets) along the physical route used for a transport connection.

Network Layer

The main function of the Network Layer is to create and maintain the logical path used by the Transport Layer. The route to be found through the network is based on its configuration (connectivity) and maybe also on other factors. Some examples of the techniques for choosing the best route through a network are:

— Fixed routeing. Fixed tables are used to find the route to a certain destination;

— Alternate path routeing. In addition to the first choice fixed route alternate routes are provided, to be used when the first choice fails;

— Dynamic or adaptive routeing. The route is established dynamically at each moment, to ensure the best use of the network resources and to minimise the transition delay of the message across the network.

The Network Layer selects each link in the network, across which the message is to be transmitted. If many messages are to be routed through the same node in the network then local congestion (at that node) may occur. This is caused by buffer allocation problems. This local congestion may spread to global congestion (across the whole of the network) if no avoiding action is taken. Alternate path routeing and dynamic (or adaptive routeing) are solutions to this problem, however even in these situations interaction may still be required with the Transport Layer to stop sending messages until the congestion has eased.

Data Link Layer

The function of the Data Link Layer is to make sure that the messages presented to it are transmitted across the link (to the next node) without errors occurring, if possible (depending on the Protocol used), during the transmission and with independence of the physical media used. Errors in the messages arise because of corruptions in the transmitted data. The corruptions can be for a number of reasons:

— Disturbances such as signal distortion, noise or switching impulses. A cyclic redundancy check may be added to the message so that the receiving terminal can conclude whether or not an error has occurred. The data is 'coded up' prior to transmission;

When a message has been received the sender must be notified if the transmission was successful. This notification of a correct or incorrect message is sent from the receiving to the sending node. The sending node will wait a specific amount of time for this positive or negative acknowledgement to be returned and during this time will have initiated a time-out. The time-out matures if the acknowledgement does not come back within the specified period. Subsequent re-transmission may now take place or if a number of time-outs have matured an error routine may be entered to say that the link is down. At this point an attempt may be made to try to re-establish the connection path. Time-outs are required because of the finite transmission time to propagate a message across the network. When re-transmissions do take place, the receiving node must be able to detect duplication, in case it is the acknowledgement and not the message that was lost. There are a number of ways of implementing time-outs and acknowledgements. It is not proposed to examine them here and the reader is referred to the references for this chapter.

Physical Layer

This the last layer of the ISO model to be considered. It is the function of this layer to translate the information to be transmitted into a physical form which can then be sent over the chosen media, eg copper wire, fibre optics, free space (microwave, radio), etc.

The media could be a network, eg for the public switched telephone network, the modem is part of the media and the V24 circuits are the Physical Layer.

The transmission media, signalling techniques and network topology are all covered in Chapter 4. It is an interesting point to note that a network management function may reside in the application layer. This function may also be distributed across the network in each node or may reside in one central node. The implications of this on network topology are obvious. Consider the discussion in Chapter 4 of star, loop and ring systems. In any case each node will hold its own well defined layers, not all necessarily in use for every transmission across the network. For example, if a node is used only as a stepping stone to get the message to its final destination then the message may only propagate up to the Network Layer of this intermediate node.

Summary and Conclusions

It is worth listing the following conclusions:

— standards are required to permit the interworking of different manufacturer's equipment;

— an 'open' network will allow the equipment of *any* manufacturer to be connected and more importantly to communicate over it;

— a 'closed' network will allow the equipment of *one* manufacturer only to be connected and to communicate over it;

— complete standards at the Application Layer will never exist because of the different requirements for specific applications. This would specify that the function keys and control characters, formats, etc used in different applications programs performed the same activities. The software investment by suppliers in applications programs also impinges on their design;

— by the same token a high investment in hardware makes it necessary to produce interfaces between individual supplier's proprietary equipment. It is here, however, in the interfaces, where OSI layered models have a strong foothold. The gateway for instance, when connected to the PTT network, *must* be 'open';

— an 'ajar' network allows connection and communication via a gateway.

OSI concepts are not new to students of telephony. In telephony these concepts take the form of CCITT recommendations. It is basically a hierarchical model. A simple summary of the layering for a network architecture is shown in Figure 5.2.

A number of network manufacturers (and indeed computer manufacturers) support not one but several ETHERNET implementations. How can this possibly tie-in with the ISO model?

The answer is – the data link and physical layers are divided vertically in order to accommodate different types of technology. The division extends into the physical medium. The data link layer is divided into two sub-layers, the Medium Access Control (MAC) layer and the Logical Link Control (LLC) layer. The MAC solves issues of contention for the medium, and its implementation is specified to the type of medium used.

The LLC is common to all media access methods with all information transfer between the Network layer and lower layers passing through it. Among the LLC's functions are Connectionless ('Datagram') Service and Connection-Oriented Service (with error correction), the Connection-Oriented Service being optional.

Because of the way the connection function is implemented, an appropriate choice of LLC cannot be made in isolation but needs to take account of user requirements and design options at other layers. The connectionless 'datagram' service contains all of the information needed to determine where it is to go within each frame. This makes for a simple LLC implementation.

There are LANs available which only support Connectionless operation and so omit the LLC altogether. The penalty of this interconnectability is constant redundant information in the transmitted frame.

LAYER	NAME	DESCRIPTION
7	APPLICATIONS	Programs to be run by end-user via his terminal
6	PRESENTATION	WHAT does the partner terminal look like?
5	SESSION	WHO is the partner terminal?
4	TRANSPORT	WHERE is the partner terminal and WHAT route is taken to achieve end-user to end-user connection? Provides a link between the device functions (Applications, Presentation and Session) and the communications functions (Network, Data and Physical).
3	NETWORK	WHICH route is taken to the partner terminal?
2	LINK	HOW is each step in the route made?
1	PHYSICAL	HOW is the physical medium used for each step?

Figure 5.2   Summary of the Layering for a Network Architecture

The ISO model thus builds up into a picture of a matrix comprising a number of options at each layer containing interfaces to different entities. The model extends in both vertical and horizontal directions.

The standards applied to LANs at the moment cover only the lower three layers of the architecture. Examples of existing standards that are widely accepted and implemented in the lower layers are RS232-C and CCITT V.24. These standards define conventional connection of data equipment and modems. An important consideration for using a layered structure is that it makes it easier to adopt the technological advances in software and hardware. These may take the form of replacing software modules or implementing hardware (eg VLSI). The impact of standards in this area affects both the user and the supplier. The standards for CSMA/CD Bus, Token Bus and Token Ring are designated under IEEE-802 standards and are 802.3, 802.4 and 802.5 respectively. At the moment only ETHERNET (802.3 – Baseband) has gained approval. There is also a standard for slotted rings, designated 802.6.

6 Choosing a Microcomputer Network

INTRODUCTION

The choice of a microcomputer network brings together all of the points discussed in the previous chapters. The procurement process can essentially be broken down into four stages:

— planning;
— specifying;
— tendering;
— installing.

Choosing the microcomputer network requires the use of feedback techniques in order to assess and refine the four stages specified above. It is essential that the stages should not be thought of as each being in isolation from the other. Isolating each stage will result at worst in not being able to install the purchased network and at best in experiencing extreme difficulty.

THE PLANNING STAGE

The first part of any planning stage is to assess the current situation. This entails evaluating the performance of the equipment currently in use or evaluating the requirement and suitability of installing new equipment.

Once again two basic situations are present which are:

— microcomputers are already being used within the environment and a decision has now been taken to network them;

— a decision has been taken to introduce a microcomputer

network into the department. The department has no previous computing experience.

Although the two points above present a different set of problems, the one common area is the identification of where the
information resides and who needs access to what. The evaluation
for both points will use interviews at some time. Interviews, with
key personnel, will help to determine both the applications and
communications software requirements. The results of the interviews provide the information to be used in forecasting future
requirements. Established data processing departments have the
benefit of drawing on a history of computer usage in order to
determine a requirement for new equipment. The personal computer user does not usually possess this history of use. Nevertheless
an effort must be made to forecast the requirements from 2 to 5
years hence, bearing in mind not only the business needs but also
the fact that the rate of change of technology is such that systems
will become less effective than newer counterparts.

The analysis of traffic patterns is important in determining the
flow of information. It is at this stage that the planner will find out
much more about the environment in which he works. The flow of
information may not merely be required within the personal computer network itself but also to external networks. Future
requirements for communications should be considered by
evaluating the company's (or department's) business strategy. This
area will have a very great impact on the enhancement path available for the chosen equipment. A decision may be made to write-
off the chosen equipment after two years, acknowledging the fact
that newer and better equipment will be available. If a decision
such as this is made, do not ignore the question of compatibility.
The cost of a useful system comprises both an initial cost and an
integrated cost. The initial cost is the visible cost of the equipment,
for example:

— workstations;
— network interfaces;
— printers (spool and quality, eg laser printer for high speed
    and daisy wheel equivalent quality;
— file servers;
— modems.

The integrated cost will need to take account of such items as:
— software development;
— program conversion;
— staff training;
— software support;
— hardware support.

The applications to which the system will be put must take into account not only the available software but also the allowable down time. This aspect of system design must be carefully thought out at the planning stage. As a business becomes more dependent on its networked systems this area becomes increasingly important.

The installation of a network is not the final stage but one of the initial stages. This may sound somewhat back-to-front; however, a network, like any other piece of equipment, if it is to be brought into use smoothly and efficiently requires planned installation. Planning must take into account geographical and architectural considerations.

Figure 6.1 provides a reference guide to some of the planning considerations.

THE SPECIFYING STAGE

Take a wide look at the available suppliers during the specifying stage. This stage presents the opportunity to bring together all of those points covered during the planning stage and relate them to suppliers' equipment.

The suppliers to be approached should be reduced to a manageable number of four to six. The suppliers may then each be approached in turn to provide demonstration visits at their premises or at the premises of a company using their equipment. Having specified the overall requirements and established that these are possible using the suppliers' proprietary equipment, the site visits should be viewed as fact finding.

Draw up a set of questions about the general system problems and application specific problems. It is important to remember that this specifying stage is the one in which thoughts are clarified as to what exactly is required. The output from the specifying stage should be a 'statement of requirements' from which the supplier can provide a tender.

The talks and visits to both suppliers and users should be used to

PLANNING CONSIDERATIONS	POINTS TO NOTE
Current Situation	equipment in use (compatibility); information flow; interviews with key end-user personnel; applications; communications (external, eg telex); employee impact
Future Situation	analysis of traffic patterns; company business policy (information flow); 2-year forecast ⎱ where 5-year forecast ⎰ appropriate enhancement path (expansion); staff training; program conversion; applications; communications (external); network response time; employee impact
Costs (visible)	hardware costs; expansion; software costs (packages)
Costs (invisible)	consumable items (paper, diskettes, ribbons, etc); staff training (user friendly system?); program conversion; system monitoring; system management
Architectural	present building (regulations); future building (alterations – system flexibility)
Geographical	network length; area coverage
System Security	master/slave required (down time); password protection

Figure 6.1　Planning Considerations

shape the 'statement of requirements'. The 'statement of requirements' will be the document used as the basis on which the suppliers will tender for the contract. Figure 6.2 lists the specifying considerations against some points to note. The specifying stage is the user's chance to ask the supplier for a system to suit his exact needs.

SPECIFYING CONSIDERATION	POINTS TO NOTE
look at the wide range of suppliers	ask for visits/demonstrations; clarify thoughts from the planning stage
clarificaton of thoughts from planning stage	reduce the numbers of suppliers to a manageable 4 to 6; produce the 'statement of requirements' output document
'STATEMENT OF REQUIREMENTS' (This document will be used as the basis of the supplier's tender)	specify present and future needs ask for details of: — hardware; — software; — communications; — costs; built around the ability of the system to function in your own environment. ask for details of: — support; — supplier's organisation; — references of companies using similar equipment; — contract terms

Figure 6.2   Specifying Considerations

THE TENDERING STAGE

The tendering stage is the point at which the supplier's proposals are evaluated. A number of the tenders can be quickly ruled out because the systems do not perform to the specifications. Individual tenders can now be followed up with a detailed examination of their performance. The points the tender should bring out are:

— cost;
— supplier support;
— supplier experience;
— system performance;
— equipment availability (off-the-shelf or delivery times quoted).

Be very wary of a supplier's promises of future developments or future enhancements. In many instances these are a long time coming. If your own company's overall business plan relies on these future enhancements then clearly the future of your company is in a network supplier's hands – a very undesirable situation. Data processing managers will be only too aware of the large computer manufacturer's promises of future products, sometimes with apparent disregard to timescale.

The suppliers should be pressed to demonstrate the relevant applications software on the same network set-up as the one that will ultimately be installed. When the final supplier has been chosen and the equipment selected, a pre-commissioning phase of the networked equipment at the supplier's premises provides an opportunity to iron out any bugs before the system is delivered. This phase is sometimes known as 'hot-staging'. Figure 6.3 highlights some points during the tendering stage.

Evaluate the architecture of the supplier's network equipment. This could range from a system with a central dedicated file server to a system that can share the resources of every station. The problem of managing the various types of network should be noted.

THE INSTALLING STAGE

The installation of the system is usually very much in the hands of the suppliers. The supplier will, however, require key information about the environment where the equipment is to be installed. This information will have been gathered during the planning stage.

Once the system has been physically installed, which in itself may require the scheduling in of several activities, for example additional mains power supplies, building alterations, etc, the

TENDERING CONSIDERATIONS	POINTS TO NOTE
Cost	— 'visible' — 'invisible' — comparison with the planning consideration costs
Supplier Support	— how much will be required by end-users? — is maintenance support included (call-out time)? — access to future or additional products
Supplier Experience	— how long has the supplier been established in the field? — have other similar networks been installed? — are references to other users supplied? — are qualified staff available?
System Performance	— stress the aspect of system not just stand-alone performance; — number of workstations supported depends on the applications the system is used for. In some cases the number of useful workstations (depending on the acceptable response time) could be as low as 5
Equipment Availability	— are the items 'off-the-shelf'? — beware of delivery time promises; — beware of development time promises

Figure 6.3 Tendering Considerations

commissioning and testing phases are entered. Commissioning the system will be performed by the supplier as will testing. However, the subsequent end-users should be brought into the testing phase at the earliest opportunity. This will ensure that software packages function and provide the intended information and in addition it will encourage end-user involvement.

The installation stage should provide for a period of joint supplier and end-user acceptance testing. The inclusion of acceptance tests will make the introduction of the system much smoother, while keeping some onus on the supplier to provide a bug-free, fully functioning system. Figure 6.4 outlines points to note during the installation stage.

INSTALLATION CONSIDERATIONS	POINTS TO NOTE
Network Equipment	— consider its suitability to the plan; — schedule in pre-installation activities; — supplier should define the time required to install the system; — building access required in order to install the system
Commissioning	— to be carried out by supplier; — access to external equipment may be required if communications software is used; — where possible this phase should be stand-alone so as not to unduly interfere with day-to-day activities
Testing	— test out the applications packages to ensure that they run; — test out the communications packages (including access to external equipment)
Acceptance	— should cover a period of joint testing; — ensure that the applications programs function in the user environment

Figure 6.4   Installation Considerations

CONCLUSIONS

The choice of a microcomputer network is far from straightfor-ward. There are often political as well as technical problems to be resolved before such a system can be implemented within a com-pany. A consultant can often provide an impartial outside view-point when company personnel may be too influenced by their personal involvement to see a problem in its true light and to propose feasible solutions. A consultant can also offer specialist expertise, especially with the technical advances progressing so rapidly.

7 The Future

The speed at which microcomputer networks proliferate in the future depends on three factors:

— the applications to which they will be put;

— the cost of the microcomputer networks;

— the standards situation.

The applications are driven both by internal and external opportunities and requirements. The internal factor, already recognised by end-users, has solutions provided by network manufacturers. The external factor has far reaching consequences for information technology with the advent, for example, of an increased number of third party information database suppliers.

The external factor brings into play wide area communications and with it the future Integrated Services Digital Network (ISDN). This network caters for voice and data utilising the digital network which at present British Telecom is introducing to replace the analogue network. Areas where ISDN will play an important role are in the industrial and commercial fields. Having to take into account future voice and data needs and the way in which these needs can be fulfilled means considering the role of the PABX and the LAN. As far as ISDN is concerned, the important point for the end-user is the network interface. For the large site the new generation of PABX systems (the Integrated Services Private Branch Exchanges, ISPBX) will use the ISDN primary rate access at 2M bit/s. The ISPBX will then offer the end-user a kind of basic access. It is possible that future personal computer networks will provide a direct connection for this basic access, designated by the CCITT as 144K bit/s. This new CCITT 1420 interface allows a number of terminals connected in a passive bus configuration to share access to two ISDN channels. It supports the full signalling capabilities of ISDN and allows line powering across the interface, meeting the ISDN requirements of both speech and data. This bus, named the S-bus, will be distributed around the office or home. It is a 4-wire bus defining the line transmission termination and hence access to ISDN (Figure 7.1). The bus can be up to 1 km in length, support up to eight terminals and will use a set of protocols similar to Ethernet. It is in this area of the small business user that ISDN will make a large impact.

Figure 7.1 shows the T reference point that marks the limit of the agreed CCITT standards.

Another advantage of ISDN is the provision of gateways to other networks, such as Packet Switch Stream (PSS). Until ISDN becomes a viable proposition, in the 1990s, users of personal computers must rely on the software and hardware suppliers to provide a private packet assembler/disassembler (PAD) function to an X.25 network, should one be required. Such packages are available now but in common with all applications software the features offered should be carefully considered. PADs do provide one solution at present to certain communications problems.

The cost of the microcomputer network does not just relate to the fact that as systems become more popular so the sales increase and the price drops. The cost reduction will come from the increasing use of Very Large Scale Integration (VLSI) techniques by chip manufacturers. VLSI will provide an impact on not only the architecture of the microcomputer but also on its ability to support certain operating systems, for example UNIX.

The UNIX operating system requires the allocation of memory resources to currently executing processes, for example the Motorola 68000, Zilog Z8000 series and Intel 80286 microprocessors support this type of function. VLSI will continue to be responsible for further advances such as the 32-bit Z80000 processor from Zilog and the 32-bit Z80386 from Intel, perhaps emerging in the next two years as common amongst personal computers.

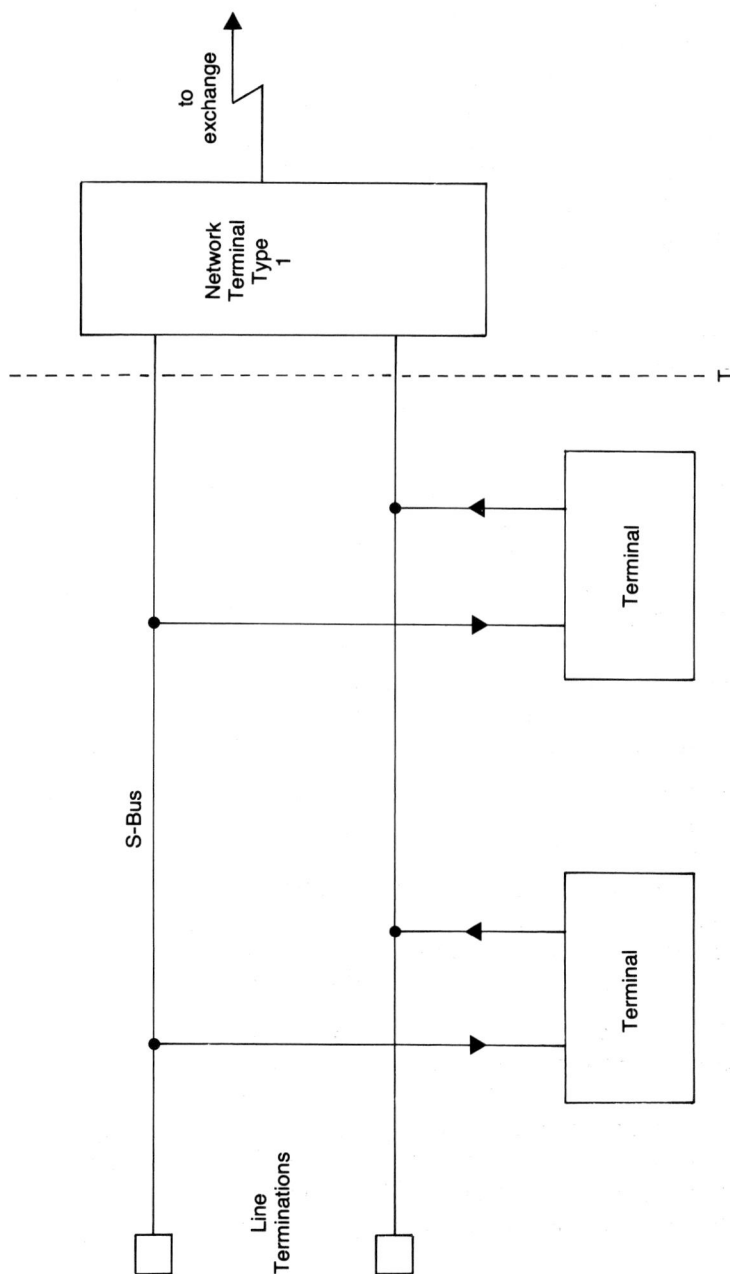

Figure 7.1 The S-bus in ISDN

The benefits of VLSI for stand-alone personal computers is very apparent as they increasingly become faster and more powerful. The benefits of VLSI for microcomputer, or personal computer, networks is yet to be fully realised. These benefits will come in the form of VLSI to support local area network access techniques. Ethernet chips are already available as general-purpose CSMA/CD controllers which are designed to come up in the Ethernet mode on power up. Families of chip sets provide the necessary Manchester encoding/decoding requirement between the CSMA/CD controller and a transceiver. The protocol design and the VLSI implementation determines the system efficiency. Bearing this in mind, it is clear why VLSI will play such an important part in the future in increasing the efficiency of a system by implementing access techniques, such as those used on buses and rings, in silicon. The resultant benefit will also be a reduced cost.

Future chip sets will be able to emulate most existing architectures through the use of microcode. The emulations may comprise the Z80 from CP/M and the 8086 for MS-DOS with UNIX as the host operating system. Such emulations are entirely feasible and are presently being employed by the NCR-32 universal emulator chip set.

The majority of microcomputer networks at present are baseband, being cheaper than its broadband counterpart. The IBM Personal Computer Network is a recent notable exception to this: it is a broadband network with a tree topology, running at 2M bits per second, having CSMA/CD as the access protocol and using 75 ohm coaxial cable as the transmission medium. The idea behind the system design will encourage third parties to develop applications such as closed circuit TV, security and teleconferencing. In using broadband technology the option is, at the moment, not a cheap one to take, however the peer-to-peer set up for the personal computers in addition to the potential use of the transmission medium will make this type of system attractive for those users willing and able to take advantage of it.

The cost of storage peripherals for a microcomputer network is also an important area as it is this resource that usually provides the best incentive to network, ie shared storage. It is possible that by 1987 erasable optical disk products will be available. Obviously the large amount of stored data will have to be balanced against the required access time. However, the systems would be most useful when used with the personal computer CAD/CAM packages now available for on-line storage and imaging. The problems concerned with access times can be alleviated by downloading the required data to local Winchester and accessing it from there.

Sharing network resources also extends to printers. The ability to share a resource often allows a single high-quality peripheral to be used instead of having to provide several lower-cost peripherals. Laser printers come under the heading of a single high-quality printer. Laser printers are able to produce output as good as a daisy wheel printer but considerably faster, approximately one page every eight seconds. A reduction in cost should make this peripheral very attractive to network users.

Microcomputers designed in the future will have the network interface built-in, although the Future Computers range of equipment, for example, has this facility built-in at present. The facility to look for in new equipment is communications. The older personal computers were not designed with communications in mind.

Future standards, although acknowledging the ISO 7-layer structure, must also take account of operating system software, proposed low-cost LANs and proposed serial interfaces for use on portable microcomputers. The British Microcomputer Manufacturer's Group, in conjunction with the Department of Trade and Industry, have drawn up a proposed low-cost LAN standard. The LAN will initially use concurrent CP/M and DR-Net from Digital Research. The standard is to support other operating systems such as BOS, MS-DOS and UNIX. It is envisaged that British information technology equipment suppliers will support this standard and that it will encourage Digital Research to achieve OSI standards.

The recognition of the fact that microcomputer networks could incorporate portable microcomputers is taken advantage of with a new proposal for an alternative interface to RS232 and Centronics. The problems with the present RS232 are:

— 25-pin D-type connectors are utilised but usually only 3 pins are used;

— the manufacturers may use male or female connectors;

— the manufacturers decide which pins they intend to use.

The proposed new low-cost interconnection for microcomputers and peripherals, put forward by the Public Services Working Party, is called the S5/8 (Serial 5-volt 8-pin) and is based on the 8-pin circular DIN socket (type 45326). The proposed S5/8 pin out is shown in Figure 7.2.

The pins are designated as:

— data in/data out;

— handshake in/handshake out;

— status in/status out;

— ground;

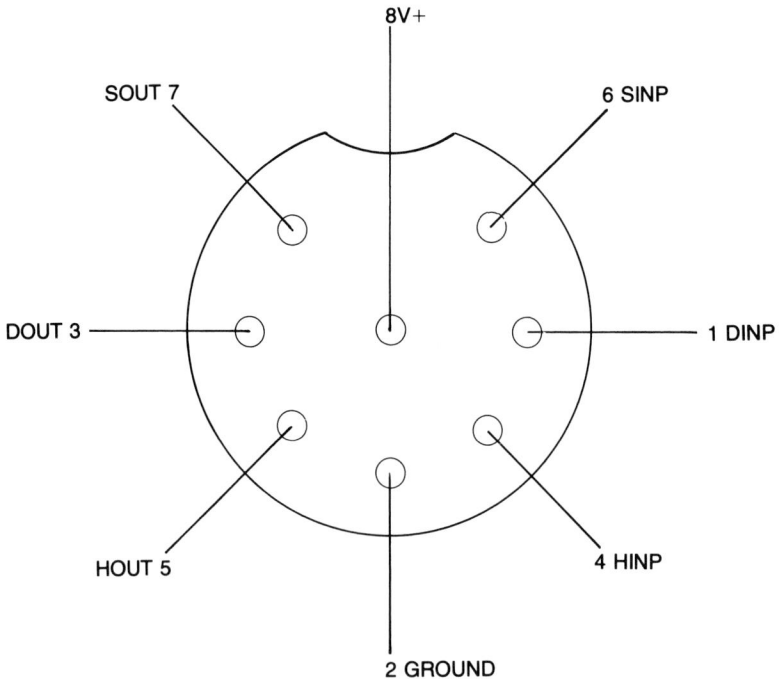

Figure 7.2   S5/8 Pin Out

— 5v power supply.

It is likely to be some time before the S5/8 interconnection gains widespread use. Its more useful application is in battery-operated portable equipment where both power and space are at a premium.

Appendix A

Product Information

The following pages provide a brief summary of some of the systems on the market. The appendix cannot cover every system on the market and it is emphasised that inclusion or exclusion by no means reflects the quality of a system. Relevant points on each product are highlighted. (More detailed product information is available from the NCC Information Desk and the NCC Hardware Directories.)

It is important to note that some of the products listed are not low-cost networks. They have been included so as to stimulate thought, as was intended throughout the book, in the areas of applications and requirements.

COMPANY	CONNECTION INFORMATION	TRANSMISSION RATE	SUPPORTS	PROPRIETARY NAME	COMMENTS
ACORN COMPUTERS	Dual twisted pair bus		BBC Computer	ECONET	Low cost network
ADVANCED NETWORK	Fibre optic/twisted pair	10 MB/s	RS232, X25	SR10	Cambridge ring
ALIQUIS COMPUTER SYSTEMS	Coaxial bus	1 MB/s	UNI/Q BUS	M-NET	
ALTOS COMPUTER SYSTEMS	Twisted pair		XENIX	TEAMNET II	8086 Systems
AMBER COMPONENTS	Ethernet coaxial	10 MB/s	PDP, VAX	3 COM	Any IEEE 796 compatible
APOLLO			Ethernet Gateway	DOMAIN	Engineering workstations
APRICOT	Twisted pair CSMA/CA	1 MB/s	MS-DOS 2.11 (in workstations)	POINT-32 (OMNINET)	32 workstations maximum
BRIDGE COMMUNICATIONS	Serial		RS232, RS423	CS1	Interface to Ethernet
BRITISH TELECOM BUSINESS SYSTEMS	Baseband token	2.5 MB/s	Concurrent DOS including IBM PC mode	M4000 Series	DATAPOINT's ARCNET
CASE	Telephone line	9.6 KB/s	RS232	GRAPEVINE	
COMART	Coaxial	10 MB/s	IBM PC	COMNET	Ethernet type

COMPANY	CONNECTION INFORMATION	TRANSMISSION RATE	SUPPORTS	PROPRIETARY NAME	COMMENTS
CORVUS (KEEN COMPUTERS)	Twisted pair RS422 CSMA	500 KB/s	via cards	OMNINET	APPLE, CONCEPT, IBM PC
CROMEMCO	Twin axial broadband	500 KB/s	S-100 bus	C-NET	Conforms to 2 lower ISO layers
DATAPOINT	Baseband coaxial			ARCNET	Token passing
DIGITAL EQUIPMENT	Coaxial		Ethernet	DECNET	Ethernet, VAX, PDP
DIGITAL MICROSYSTEMS	Twisted pair, screened multi-way	500 KB/s	IBM PC, APRICOT	HINET	32 workstations maximum
DOXIVER	Baseband CSMA coaxial	1 MB/s	MS-DOS	PC-NET	
ENCOTEL			TELEVIDEO	MMMOST	
GANDALF DIGITAL	Coaxial		IBM 3270	PACXNET	
GE (USA)	Broadband	1/5 MB/s	RS232C, IEEE	GE-NET	20 channels
HASLER	Coaxial			SILK	Ring
HAWKER SIDDELEY	Multilink ring	250 KB/s	APPLE DEC	MULTILINK	125 Micros
HEWLETT PACKARD			HP9000	HP2285A	Ethernet type
HYTEC MICROSYSTEMS				TECNET	Ethernet type

COMPANY	CONNECTION INFORMATION	TRANSMISSION RATE	SUPPORTS	PROPRIETARY NAME	COMMENTS
IBM	Broadband, coaxial CSMA/CD	2 MB/s		PC Network	Single cable broadband
ICE	Ribbon (multiway)	600 KB/s	IBM, SIRIUS	LATTICE	APPLE
ICL	Coaxial	1 MB/s		MICROLAN	Primary node and up to 16 secondary
INTEL		10 MB/s	IEEE 802	82586	Built in diagnostics
INTERNET LTD	Baseband coaxial	1 MB/s	RS232C	INTERNET	
KEEN COMPUTERS	34 way ribbon	60 KB/s	IBM, APPLE	CONSTELLA	SIRIUS OSBORNE
LOGICA VTS	Twisted pair, ring			POLYNET	Cambridge ring
LSI	Baseband, coaxial tree	2.5 MB/s	CP/M, DrNet	LSI NET	Based on ARCNET (for OCTOPUS systems)
MASTER SYSTEMS	Multiway, twisted pair ring	10 MB/s	CP/M Emulation	XINET	Range of network options
MICRODATA	Coaxial	2 MB/s	Series 8000 IBM PC	NEWLAN	up to 5 km
MODATA COMPUTERS	Twisted pair	500 KB/s	IBM, SIRIUS	MICROMAST	APPLE, OSBORNE, RAINBOW
MODUS SYSTEMS			TENSOR MICRO	MODUS	Industrial and factory automation
NEC BUSINESS SYSTEMS	Coaxial daisy chain	625 KB/s	CP/M	QDOS	

COMPANY	CONNECTION INFORMATION	TRANSMISSION RATE	SUPPORTS	PROPRIETARY NAME	COMMENTS
NETWORK SYSTEMS	Coaxial	50 MB/s	IBM, DEC	HYPERCHAN	also Honeywell and Burroughs support
NINETILE COMPUTERS	Twisted pair, ring	10 KB/s	RS232C/V24	MULTILINK	EPSON, APPLE
PLESSEY	Cluster	1.8 MB/s	MSDOS, CP/M 86	IWS III CLUSTER	
PLEXUS COMPUTERS	Ethernet	10 MB/s	IBM PLEXUS	PLEXUS	PLEXUS P/35, P/40, P/60
POSITRONIKA	Coaxial	2.5 MB/s	PDP Q-BUS	BUDGETNET	Q-BUS and UNIBUS on one board
PRIME	Coaxial, ring	8 MB/s		PRIME 50	Concurrent high speed communications
QUORUM COMPUTERS	Coaxial	4/10 MB/s	CP/M	QUORUMNET	up to 64 workstations
RACAL-MILGO	Ring	10 MB/s		PLANET	Reconfigurable ring
REAL TIME DEVELOPMENTS	Coaxial, ring	10 MB/s	RS232	CLEARWAY	
RECOGNITION EQUIPMENT	Bus parallel	6.4 MB/s	CP/M	TARTAN	16 set bus expandable 3270/3780
RESEARCH MACHINES	Coaxial CSMA/CD	0.8 MB/s	MS DOS	CHAIN	64 workstations maximum opto isolation
RIVA TERMINALS	Coaxial	56 KB/s	RS232 IBM PC	LANYARD	

COMPANY	CONNECTION INFORMATION	TRANSMISSION RATE	SUPPORTS	PROPRIETARY NAME	COMMENTS
SYMBIOTIC	Fibre optic		DOS, CP/M	SYMBNET	up to 9 km
SYTEK	Broadband bus, coaxial	2 MB/s		LOCAL-NET	Ethernet type
TESCO	Coaxial	2.5 MB/s	IBM PC	MULTINET	
TOLTEC	Twin twisted pair cables	10 MB/s		DATARING	up to 16 workstations
TORCH COMPUTERS	Dual twisted pair, bus (tree)	50 KB/s/330 KB/s	PRESTEL, ICL	TORCHNET	ECONET plus higher level
TORUS	Ethernet	10 MB/s	IBM PC	ICON NETWORK	up to 100 workstations
TRIUMPH ADLER			CP/M	MICRONITE	Single user
UNGERMANN-BASS	Coaxial	10 MB/s	RS232C	NET-ONE	also broadband, fibre optic
VECTOR GRAPHIC INCORPORATED	Twisted pair, token ring	750 KB/s	CP/M	LINC	
WANG	(Broadband)			WANGNET	
XEROX	Coaxial	10 MB/s	DIGITAL EQUIPMENT	ETHERNET	up to 2.5 km maximum
XIONICS LTD.				XINET	
ZILOG	Coaxial	800 KB/s	ZILOG 8000	Z NET	Link to UNIX
ZYNAR	Straight line bus	250 KB/s	UCSD CP/M	CLUSTER ONE	
ZYNAR	Coaxial	2.5 MB/s	IBM PC	PLAN/2000	

Appendix B

Glossary

Access method
The mechanism used to share a common physical transmission medium between a number of users.

Analogue transmission
Transmission of a continuously variable signal.

Application program generator (APG)
A method of creating applications software by automating some of the development work.

Applications layer, OSI
The highest layer defined by the ISO Reference Model concerned with providing services to applications programs which exchange information with others.

Arithmetic checksum
Character or characters added to a block of data based on some arithmetic property of this block which is used for error detection.

Arithmetic and logic unit (ALU)
The part of the Central Processing Unit (CPU) handling arithmetic and logic operations.

Asynchronous transmission
Transmission in which there is no fixed time interval between characters. The start of a character is marked by a start signal and the character is terminated by a stop signal.

Bandwidth   The range of frequencies available for signalling in a communications channel.

Baseband signalling   Transmission of a signal at its original frequencies, ie unmodulated.

Basic input/output system (BIOS)   That part of the system responsible for controlling the hardware for inputting and outputting data.

Baud rate   The unit of discrete signalling speed per second; the modulation rate. The baud rate is equivalent to bits per second only if each signal represents exactly one bit.

Bit   Abbreviation of binary digit. The signal element of transmission in binary notation which can take the two values '0'(OFF) or '1'(ON).

Bit rate   The number of bits transferred in unit time, usually expressed in bits per second (bps).

Break-out box   A device which can be inserted in a serial transmission line to enable the signal levels to be monitored and cross-connections to be made.

Bridge   A device used to connect similar networks together.

British standards institution (BSI)   Institution responsible for generating and promoting standards.

Broadband signalling   Transmission of a signal at a frequency higher than the original, ie modulated. Many signals will usually be carried by the same transmission medium by occupying separate frequency bands.

Buffer insertion   (*See* Register insertion)

Bus	A single common data highway shared by a number of devices.
Byte	A sequence of bits, normally eight, which represents one character.
Byte stuffing	A method of obtaining data transmission transparency by inserting special prefix characters to mark modified characters.
Carrier sense multiple access (CSMA)	A method of sharing a common data highway by testing whether the highway is in use before transmission. To avoid the problem of two stations trying to transmit at the same time, collision avoidance (CSMA/CA) or collision detection (CSMA/CD) techniques are usually adopted.
Central processing unit (CPU)	The central part of a computer which includes all the major control and arithmetic units, with the exception of memory and peripheral interfaces.
Character set	The set of letters, figures, punctuation and control codes in a message. Each character is usually represented by one byte.
Check bit or check character	A bit or character associated with a character or block of characters for error detection purposes.
Circuit switching	Conventional interconnection where a two-way fixed bandwidth circuit is allocated exclusively to the parties concerned for the duration of the call.
Computer aided design (CAD)	Computer usage to assist design, often combined with CAM.
Computer aided manufacture (CAM)	Computer usage to assist manufacture, often combined with CAD.

Computer automated management and control standard (CAMAC)
BSI standard covering all communications from component level up.

Concentrator
A device that provides communications facilities between a number of low-speed devices and one or more high-speed channels.

Concurrency
Availability of a number of services or applications at the same time.

Connectivity
The flexibility of a network in providing connections to a number of different systems.

Contention
An access method which relies on competition for a shared data highway.

Control codes
A non-printable character whose function is to initiate, modify or stop a control operation.

Critical path analysis
Method of project control highlighting activities critical to project completion, often used with PERT.

Cyclic redundancy check
A method used to detect errors in transmitted data by adding a string of specially constructed check characters to the data.

Data buffering
The storage of data characters for speed matching or interfacing purposes.

Data communications equipment (DCE)
In data networks, a DCE is any device used to interface the data terminal equipment (DTE) to the communications line.

Data link layer,
OSI
The layer defined by the ISO Reference Model concerned with ensuring transmission errors across a data link are detected and corrected.

Data link protocol
A set of rules used to ensure that transmission errors across a data link are detected and corrected. High Level Data Link Control is a typical example.

Data switch
A circuit switching system designed to carry data exclusively.

Data terminal
equipment (DTE)
In a data network, a DTE is any device attached to the network which originates data or is a destination device for data.

Database
An organised collection of data available to a number of users.

Digital transmission
This is the transmission of data characters by coding into discrete signals.

Direct memory access
(DMA)
Method of accessing memory without using the main processor.

Direct memory access
controller (DMAC)
Hardware responsible for controlling the direct memory access.

Distributed computing
An arrangement of computing facilities where a number of computers are spread around a site with high-speed interconnecting links for resource sharing.

Echo
The display of a character keyed in at a terminal. The displayed character may be routed from the keyboard to the screen locally or may be transmitted from the remote computer.

Editor
A program, usually supplied with the computer, for the creation of text files.

Electronic mail   A service for the transfer of documents between computer users attached to a network.

Empty slot   (*See* Slotted ring)

Encryption   The encoding of data into a new form which needs a specific algorithm to decipher it.

Error rate   The probability, within a given sample size of bits, characters or blocks, of one being in error.

Field   Part of a group of characters with special significance.

File   A logical organisation of characters or data, stored on the computer memory, disk, tape or other storage medium.

Filter   Another name for a bridge, a device for linking similar networks.

Fixed slot   A network access method which gives each node on a ring a slot for its exclusive use.

Floppy disk   A computer storage medium which uses a thin flexible disk, usually 8 inches or $5\frac{1}{4}$ inches in diameter, to store digital data.

Flow control   A mechanism for ensuring that characters can be exchanged between two devices in an orderly manner without loss.

Frame   A group of characters containing several fields which form a single message.

Frequency division multiplexing   A method of sharing a transmission line by dividing the available bandwidth into a number of smaller bandwidth channels.

Front-end processor   A special-purpose computer dedicated to handling the communications needs of a number of terminals connected to a host computer.

Full duplex   Simultaneous transmission of data between two devices in both directions.

Gateway   A device for interconnecting dissimilar networks.

Half duplex   Transmission of data between two devices in both directions, but not simultaneously.

Host   A central computer system which can run applications for users connected via a computer network.

Hunt group   Facilities which are accessed by a queuing mechanism.

Input/output device   Any device such as a keyboard or printer which can be used to enter data into a computer or read data from a computer.

Integrated services digital network (ISDN)   Digital network being introduced by British Telecom to cater for voice and data requirements.

Integrated services private branch exchange (ISPBX)   New generation PABX using the ISDN primary rate access.

Interchange circuit   The term used by the CCITT for inter-connecting circuits at the interface between terminals (DTE) and modems (DCE).

International standards organisation (ISO)   International standards body responsible for the 7-layer reference model.

Interrupt

A computer hardware feature which allows a low-priority operation to be temporarily suspended to enable a high-priority operation to be carried out.

Interworking

The ability to exchange data between computers from different suppliers.

Invertible file transfer

A file transfer from one machine to another and back again without loss of any attributes.

Kilo bits per second (KB/s)

Thousand bits per second

Large scale integration (LSI)

Method of implementing more than one circuit (or computer) component on a single chip.

Leased line

A rented telephone circuit which provides a permanent connection between two points.

Local area network

A communications network limited to a small area, usually a single site.

Logical link control (LLC)

Sub-layer of the data link layer of the ISO reference model. Responsible for connectionless and connection-oriented service.

Macro

A group of instructions or table of data which can be inserted in a program using a single name.

Mailbox

Part of the storage in an electronic mail service which hold the documents for one user.

Mainframe

A large computer system, designed to carry out high-speed data processing.

Manchester encoding

A signalling scheme which also carries clocking information.

Medium access control (MAC)

Sub-layer of the data link layer of the ISO reference model. Responsible for solving issues of contention for the medium.

Mega bits per second (MB/s)

Million bits per second.

Microcomputer

A small computer designed for personal use.

Micronet

A local area network for microcomputers.

Microprocessor

A large-scale integrated circuit providing the control and arithmetic functions which form part of a complete microcomputer.

Minicomputer

A medium-sized computer capable of supporting departmental needs with a number of interactive terminals.

Modem

Abbreviation for modulator/demodulator, a device which converts digital information into an analogue form suitable for transmission over the analogue telephone network. The modem also performs the reverse function.

Multi-drop

A network configuration in which the central system communicates successively with a number of attached terminals. (*See* Polled network)

Multiplexing

A mechanism for carrying a number of low-speed data signals over one high-speed channel.

Network layer, OSI

The layer defined by the ISO Reference Model concerned with the routing and switching operations associated with the establishment and

	maintenance of a connection between systems.
Null-modem cable	A cable which allows two terminals to communicate over a V.24 serial line by simulating the presence of modems and a telephone line.
Open systems interconnection (OSI)	Standardisation procedures which allow terminals, computers and other devices from different suppliers to exchange data.
Operating system	Software which provides all the basic services required to run applications programs, handle input/output devices and manage the storage medium for a computer.
Packet assembler/ disassembler (PAD)	A device which forms the serial data stream from a simple terminal into packets for transmission across a packet switching network. The PAD also performs the reverse function.
Packet switch stream (PSS)	UK public packet switch service
Packet switching	A method of carrying data across a data transmission network in blocks with a defined format containing control and data fields. Each packet carries information which allows the packet switching exchanges to route it to its destination without a permanent circuit being maintained.
Parity bit	A non-information bit which is added to the bits forming a character to help detect transmission errors. The parity bit is added such that the resulting number of 1s in the group is odd (odd parity) or even (even parity).

Peripheral interchange program (PIP)
A utility program which allows the transfer of files between the peripherals attached to a computer. A number of facilities are usually provided for the user such as converting upper-case letters to lower-case, or vice versa, and filtering form feeds from the source file.

Physical layer, OSI
The layer defined by the ISO Reference Model concerned with the interface to the cable and the control of its use.

Point-to-point
A network in which pairs of end points are connected by a direct link.

Polled network
A type of network in which each channel is periodically interrogated to determine if it is active.

Postal, telegraph and telephone authority (PTT)
Public authority responsible for providing the services of post, telegraph and telephone. Extends also to data.

Presentation layer, OSI
The layer defined by the ISO Reference Model concerned with the two-way function of taking information from applications and converting it into a form suitable for a common, machine-independent understanding.

Private automatic branch exchange (PABX)
Telephone exchange used on a company's premises to provide an interface between the company's employees and the external telephone network.

Programmable interrupt controller (PIC)
Controller to handle multiple interrupt lines.

Programmable interval timer (PIT)
Piece of hardware to generate program delays.

Project evaluation and review technique (PERT)
Method of controlling a project. Often used with critical path analysis.

Proprietary network architecture
A network structure which has been designed by a single supplier, and is therefore under the supplier's complete control.

Protocol
A set of rules governing the format and exchange of data between two devices such that reliable communication is maintained.

Protocol converter
A device which enables communication between equipment using different protocols, by effecting conversion between the protocols.

Public switched telephone network (PSTN)
Telephone network provided by a PTT or private company.

Random access memory (RAM)
A type of memory element and structure which allows individual elements to be written to or read from.

Read only memory (ROM)
A permanent memory structure which can only be read from. Some types of read only memory (EPROM) can be reprogrammed using special equipment.

Record
The first major unit in a database which can be uniquely identified. Each record contains a number of individual data values or fields.

Register insertion
A type of ring network access method which requires repeaters that have a buffer which can be switched in and out of the circuit as required.

Repeater
A device inserted into a transmission

line to restore the waveform and amp-
litude of a signal.

Response time   The time between sending the last
character of a message from a terminal
to the receipt of the first character of
the reply. It includes terminal delay,
network delay, and host computer
delay.

Serial interface   The circuitry which allows each bit in a
string of characters to be sent sequen-
tially along a single channel.

Serial transmission   The transmission of data in which each
bit is transferred along a single chan-
nel sequentially rather than simultaneously as in parallel transmission.

Server   A device connected to a network
which provides a service, such as
printer spooling, to the devices
attached to the network.

Session layer, OSI   The layer defined by the ISO Reference Model concerned with the trans-
fer of data between two applications.
The two applications form a liaison for
this purpose, known as a session.

Signalling   The modification of some transmission characteristic to carry informa-
tion.

Slotted ring   A network access method where one
or more packets circulate continu-
ously around a ring.

Speed matching   The connection of two devices operating at different baud rates.

Statement of requirements   Document prepared by the prospec-
(SOR)   tive purchaser of a system for sub-
mission to a possible supplier.

Star network

A type of network topology which has a central hub with links radiating out from it.

Statistical multiplexer

An intelligent time-division multiplexer that has unequal time slots to maximise the utilisation of transmission capacity.

Synchronous transmission

A transmission technique in which data is sent without start and stop bits between characters at the start of transmission. A special group of characters is sent to synchronise the receiver with the incoming data stream.

Telephone circuit

A communications link, characterised by limited bandwidth (300Hz to 3,400Hz) and poor noise and interference properties, designed to carry speech traffic.

Teletex

A public document transfer service with a large character set.

Teletype

An early electromechanical computer terminal, operating at slow speeds, with upper-case only characters.

Telex

A well-established public document transfer service with a limited character set and low transmission speed.

Terminal concentrator

A device which allows a number of low-speed terminals to share one or more high-speed channels.

Terminal emulator

Software which allows a microcomputer to perform like a proprietary computer terminal.

Time division multiplexing

A technique of dividing the transmission capacity of a line into time slots

	which can be allocated to a number of channels.
Token passing	A ring network access method which utilises a special packet or token that is passed from one user to another and grants the holder of it the exclusive use of the network.
Transmission mode	The kind of signalling used to carry data over a transmission line.
Transparency	A communications link is said to be transparent if it allows the transfer of all characters without altering the message or taking control action.
Transport layer, OSI	The layer defined by the ISO Reference Model concerned with the provision of a particular class and quality of transmission. The transport layer is responsible for optimising the available resources to provide this service.
Tree network	A type of network topology in which the data highways can branch a number of times before reaching the nodes.
V-series recommendations	The CCITT recommendations for data transmission over telephone (ie analogue) circuits.
Value added network	A network which provides services in addition to simple connections, such as protocol conversion and network management.
Videotex	Public information service which can be accessed via a modified television receiver or special terminal connected to an ordinary telephone line.

Very large scale integration (VLSI)

Next step up from LSI, often implementing a computer on a single chip.

Virtual circuit

A connection between devices which uses a virtual circuit appears to be a permanent physical circuit to the users, but in reality it is shared by other users and may involve more than one physical route.

Wide area network

A communications network which can extend to a global scale, involving the use of circuits provided by various PTTs.

Winchester disk

A storage medium which achieves high storage density and data transfer rate by sealing rigid disks in an evacuated enclosure.

Word length

The size in bits of the internal computer registers and data highways.

Workstation

Equipment based on the microcomputer which provides a wide range of services for the electronic office environment.

X-series recommendations (eg, X25)

The CCITT recommendations for data transmission over public data networks.

References and Bibliography

CHAPTER 1

Banks M, The oem micro, *Systems International*, May 1984, pp 95-96

Earnshaw M C, Networks for data and computer communications – the view from europe, *Telecommunications*, February 1984, pp 65-67

Gawdun M, Networks for data and computer communications – an american view, *Telecommunications*, February 1984, pp 57-70

Hogers H P, Local area networks, *Canadian Datasystems*, July 1984, pp 41-45

Horwitt E, Looking for the promised lan, *Business Computer Systems*, June 1984, pp 112-146

Marion L, The dp budget survey: pcs make waves, *Datamation*, April 1984, pp 82-89

Mayne A J, *Linked Local Area Networks*, October Press, 1982

CHAPTER 2

Horton F W, Information, resources, management: concept and cases, *Association for Systems Management*, Cleveland, Ohio, 1979

Janjua M S, Network analysis on the micro, *Computer Systems*, August 1984, pp 43-48

Kornstein H, Graphics interface for the pc, *Systems International*, December 1984, pp 68-69

McLuckie I, Advanced communications for sheltered housing, *Electronics and Power*, May 1984, pp 374-378

Seaman A, CAD-CAM on micros – not just child's play, *Computer Systems*, January 1985, pp 51-53

CHAPTER 3

Baum P, Catch the IEEE-488 bus, *Microcomputing*, April 1984, pp 116-118

Chard R A, *Evaluating Program Generators for Micros*, NCC Publications, 1985

Feldman S, Flight info, *Systems International*, January 1985, pp 22-23

Gandy M, *Microcomputer Communications*, NCC Publications, 1985

Howarth R, UCSD p-system – a review, *Microsoftware*, November 1982, pp 29-31

Jackson G, Maximising multibus, *Systems International*, June 1984, pp 51-52

Pritchard J A T, *Security In On-Line Systems*, NCC Publications, 1979

Rolander T, CP/Net acts as bridge in shared information network, *Practical Computing*, February 1981, pp 76-77

Scott P R D, *Reviewing Your Data Transmission Network*, NCC Publications, 1983

CHAPTER 4

Gee K C E, *Local Area Networks*, NCC Publications, 1982

Hall M, Broadband local area networks, *Telecommunications*, December 1983, pp 65-68

Hull J A, Characterisation of transmission media, *Telecommunications*, February 1984, pp 70-72

MicroSystems Centre, *Evolution Of Local Networks*, NCC Publications, Special Report

CHAPTER 5

BSI, *CSMA/CD Local Area Networks*, Part 1 Technical Specification, 1984

Gee K C E, *Local Area Networks*, NCC Publications, 1982

Joint Network Team, *Cambridge Ring 82 Protocol Specification*

CHAPTER 6

Beaman I R, *Small Business Computers For First Time Users*, NCC Publications, 1983

Williamson S L, *Selecting Small Business Systems*, NCC Publications, 1983

Index

access control   26
(*See also* accessibility *and*
security)
accessibility   93
(*See also* access control *and*
security)
acknowledgements   136
'ajar' network   137
amplifier   90
APPLE DOS
See personal computer
operating systems
application layer   132
application program generators   69, **73**, 74
arithmetic and logic unit   49
availability   47, 93, **95**

baseband   87, 105, **119**
(*See also* Manchester encoding)
BASIC   74
BDOS   82
BIOS   82
BOS
See personal computer
operating systems
bridges   **27**, 36, 40, 69

British Microcomputer
  Manufacturer's Group   155
broadband   87, 104, **120**
BT Gold   39
  (*See also* message distribution)
buffering   26
bus
  See parallel interface

cabling   **87, 88, 89, 90**
CCITT 1420 interface   152
CCITT V24/V35
  See serial interface
  (*See also* Consultative Committée
  Internationale Telephonique et
  Telegraphique)
central filing system   37
central processor unit   47, 49
channel spacing   19
checklists
  See summaries
checksum   60
choosing a network   25, 49
circuit switched data network   20
clock   47
'closed' network   137
communications   33, 77, **84, 85**
community services   42
computer aided design and
  manufacture   43, 155
concurrent CP/M
  See personal computer
  operating systems
congestion   21
connectionless service   138
connection-oriented service   138
consultant   149
Consultative Committée Internationale
  Telephonique et Telegraphique   129

contention   26
co-processor   49, **52**
corporate information   36, 70, 91
CP/M 8/16 bit
    See personal computer
    operating systems
critical path analysis   44
cross-talk   19, 104
current loop interface
    See serial interface
cyclic redundancy check   60

data circuit terminating
    equipment   62
data link layer   135
data networks
    — circuit switched   20
    — message switched   20
    — packet switched   21
data processing department   74
data terminal equipment   62
database   17, **39**, 40, 41, 84, 151
database access   39
datagram
    see connectionless service
development systems   41
diagnostics   96
direct addressing   47
direct memory access   49, **58**
direct memory addressing   47
direct memory addressing
    controller   53, 58
DR-Net
    See network operating systems

education   42
electronic mail
    See message distribution
electronic message system   37
    (*See also* message distribution)

electronic publishing   41
Ethernet   66, 137, 139, 152, 154
    (*See also* network access and
    sharing techniques (carrier
    sense multiple access with
    collision detection))   66, 137, 139, 152, 154
expansion chassis   49, 66
external facilities   33, 84

file locking   39
file server   23, 70, 73, 82

gateways   **26**, 36, 39, 69, 84, 137
guard band   19
guided media   100
    — coaxial cable   104
    — multi-way cable   103
    — optical fibre   109, 128
    — twisted-pair cable   100
    (*See also* transmission media)

hardware   45
head-end   90, 120
hierarchical structure   12, 15
'hot-staging'   146

IBM personal computer network   154
IBM's SNA
    See protocol
ICL's CO3
    See protocol
IEEE-488 bus   40, **64**
    (*See also* interface buses)
IEEE-802
    See standards
IEEE S100
    See interface buses
industrial systems   40
information management system   33

information retrieval   39, 42
  (*See also* database)
input/output   47, 53, **56**
  (*See also* polling, interrupt
  and direct memory access)
input/output interface
  See Universal Asynchronous/
  Synchronous Receiver Transmitter
installation   **86, 146**
instructions   47
integrated operating systems
  See personal computer
  operating systems
integrated service private
  branch exchange   151
integrated services digital
  network   27, 151
Intel
  —   8086   56
  —   80286   152
  —   80386   152
Intel Multibus
  See interface buses
interconnectability   37
interface buses   61, **63**
  (*see also* serial interface
  and parallel interface)
International Gateway Exchange   12
International Standards Organisation
  —   7-layer model   66, 131, 155
  —   application layer   132
  —   data link layer   135
  —   network layer   134
  —   physical layer   136
  —   presentation layer   132
  —   session layer   133
  —   transport layer   133
interrupt   56

large scale integration   49

laser printers   155
load curve   41
local area networks   11, **22**
logical link control   137
loosely-coupled system   53

mainframe   15, 36, 84, 89
maintainability   94
Manchester encoding   120, 154
  (*See also* baseband)
medical applications   42
medium access control   137
memory   47, 53
message distribution   31
message switched data
  network   20
microcomputer   15
microcomputer networks
  See personal computer networks
microprocessors
  —   8-bit   24, 52, 78
  —   16-bit   24, 52, 78, 152
  —   32-bit   24, 152
  (*See also* Intel, Motorola,
  NCR, Zilog *and* summaries)
minicomputer   15
modulation   19
modulator-demodulator   18, 66, 68, 130
Motorola 68000   152
MSDOS
  See personal computer operating
  systems
multiplex hierarchy   19
multi-user   70, 78

network access and sharing
  techniques   79, 99, **117**
  —   broadcast bus   124
  —   carrier sense multiple access
      with collision avoidance   125

— carrier sense multiple access
  with collision detection   125, 154
— empty slot   125
— fixed slot   125
— frequency division multiplexing   122
  (See also polling)
— time division multiplexing   122
— token passing   124
network analysis   43
  (See also critical path analysis
  and project evaluation and
  review technique)
network configuration   86
  (See also network topologies)
network control   26
network layer   134
network management   26
  (See also network operation)
network operating systems   **79**, 155
network operation   91
  (See also network management)
network topologies   79, 99
— bus/highway   116
— loop   115
— mesh   111, 114
— ring   116
— star   114
  (See also network configuration)
non-personal information access   32

OASIS
  See personal computer operating
  systems
'open' network   137
Open Systems Interconnection
  See International Standards
  Organisation, 7-layer model
operating systems
  See network operating systems

and personal computer
  operating systems
optical disk   42, 154
optical transmission system   105
  — detectors   107
  — sources   106

packet assembler/disassembler
  (PAD)   152
Packet Switch Stream   152
packet switched data network   21
parallel interface   62
parity   60, 84
partition   70
passwords
  See security
personal computer networks   11, **24**, 39
personal computer operating
  systems   **75**, 152, 154, 155
  (*See also* summaries)
personal information management   32
physical layer   136
PICK
  See personal computer operating
  systems
planning   141
polling   **56**, 115, **122**
ports   66, 84
postal, telegraph and telephone
  authority (PTT)   17, 18, 137
presentation layer   132
PRESTEL   18
primary switching centre   15
print server   23
private automatic branch
  exchange   11, 15, 17, 114, 151
private network   20
programmable interrupt controller   53
programmable interval timer   53

project evaluation and
  review technique   44
protocol   26, 84
Public Services Working
  Party   156
public switched telephone
  network   18
pyramid structure   12

radio frequency sweep
  generator   87
random access memory
  See memory
read only memory
  See memory
real-time system   41
record locking   39, **70**, **72**, 75, **83**
recovery   93, **94**
register set   49
reliability   40, 93, **94**
requestor   82
resiliency   93
response time   47, 73
return loss   87
route selection   26
RS232C/RS422
  See serial interface

S5/8 standard   156
S-bus   152
security   40, 83, **93**, 96
  — access control   26
  — accessibility   93
  — recovery   93, 94
  — reliability   40, 93, 94
  — resiliency   93
semaphore   72
serial interface   61, **62**, 139, 155
servers   82

— file   23, 70, 73, 82
— print   23
session layer   133
shared facilities   33
signalling   11
single user packages   69
specifying   143
splitter   90
SS50
    See interface buses
standards   **129**, 139, 151
statement of requirements   144
store and forward
    See buffering
summaries
— cable installation   89
— communications software
      requirements   85
— hardware   68
— installation procedure   92, 148
— microprocessor features   48
— network access and
      sharing methods   126, 127
— network architecture   138
— networks   29
— operation and management
      requirements   97
— personal computer operating
      systems   80,81
— planning   144
— specifying   145
— tendering   147
— topologies   118
— transmission media   112, 113
switching   11, 26
System X   20, 27

tap   90
telephone network   12
tendering   146

text preparation   31, 56
tightly-coupled system   53
time-out   136
traffic analysis   96
transmission   11, 128
transmission media   79, 99, **100**
   (*See also* guided media
   and unguided media)
transport layer   133

UCSD p-system
   See personal computer
   operating systems
unguided media   111
   (*see also* transmission media)
Universal Asynchronous
   Receiver Transmitter   58, 60
Universal Synchronous
   Receiver Transmitter   58, 61
UNIX
   See personal computer operating
   systems
user-friendly   67, **74**, 87

very large scale integration   22, 139, 152, 154
videotex   40, 42
viewdata   40, 41, 42
VME bus
   See interface buses

wide area networks   11, **17**, 22
word processing
   See text preparation
workstation   **32**, 36

X.25   152
XENIX
   See personal computer operating
   systems

Zilog
   —   Z8000   152
   —   Z80000   152